Audrey Cohen College

5 0664 01006070 7

Y0-CTG-634

LB
1620.52
A4
A44
1990

DATE DUE

DEMCO

Teaching Cases in Cross-Cultural Education

No. 7

Cross-Cultural Counseling:
The Guidance Project and the Reluctant Seniors

Arthur W. Allen, III

Edited by Judith Kleinfeld
Center for Cross-Cultural Studies
College of Rural Alaska
University of Alaska Fairbanks

Cross-Cultural Counseling: The Guidance Project and the Reluctant Seniors

© 1990 Judith Kleinfeld

Mr. Allen is an Alaskan rural teacher and has prepared this case on the basis of his experience in different rural communities. The village and students described are composites. In one or two cases, where a prominent figure might be recognized, his or her permission for inclusion in this case has been given.

Elmer E. Rasmuson Library Cataloging-in-Publication Data

Allen, Arthur W. III
    Cross-cultural counseling: The guidance project and the reluctant seniors.

    (Teaching cases ; no.7)

    1. Student counselors—Alaska—Case studies. 2. Vocational guidance—Case studies. 3. Personnel service in education—Alaska—Case studies. I. University of Alaska Fairbanks. Center for Cross-Cultural Studies. II. Title. III. Series: Teaching cases in cross-cultural education; no. 7.

LB1620.5.A45 1990
ISBN 1-877962-15-5

Contents

Introduction v
List of Characters xi

Part I: Background and Context

The Guidance Project 3
Fred Young and His Background 5
The Yup'ik Community of Tutuluq 6

Part II: Reluctant Seniors

Fred Young as Site Guidance Counselor 11
The Itinerant Counselor from Mountain and Valley School District 20
Last Year's Seniors 21
The District In-Service Meeting on Guidance 25
The Third Guidance Session 29
The Staff Meeting 31

Part III: The Guidance Project

January Arrives and the Guidance Project Begins 37
The Next Week 41
Deadlines Approaching 42
Epilogue: The Graduating Seniors 45

Discussion Questions 46

Supplementary Materials

1. Rural Students and the Transition to Adulthood 51
2. College Entrance Rates in Alaska by Ethnicity and Gender 56
3. Participation of Inupiat Men and Women in the Wage Economy ... 57
4. Counseling Programs in Small Rural High Schools 66
5. Broaden Students' Experience with Travel Programs 69
6. University Programs that Assist Rural High School Students 74

Introduction

Cross-Cultural Counseling: The Guidance Project and the Reluctant Seniors describes a rural Alaska high school teacher's earnest and intense efforts to motivate his nine Yup'ik seniors to plan for their futures after high school. The teacher, Fred Young, wants his students to go on to college or vocational school. He takes on the difficult position of "site guidance counselor," adding the additional responsibilities of this role—whatever these might be—to the already heavy teaching load of a small high school teacher.

What is the proper role of a school guidance counselor in a small Yup'ik community? Fred Young worries whether he is pushing his students too much, whether his aspirations for them, indeed his very emphasis on planning for the future, conflict with Yup'ik values and ways of life. Some of the village elders, he has heard, tell his students in the Yup'ik language that "school is for nothing." What is the village high school supposed to be preparing students for—the Yup'ik community or the world outside the village? How can the school prepare students for college and careers and at the same time help to maintain the Yup'ik culture?

The case describes Fred's efforts to develop a guidance program, how he pins his hopes on a special two-week guidance project, the results of this project, and what finally happens to his Yup'ik seniors in the year after high school.

Cross-Cultural Counseling is not simply a narrative, one teacher's story. Nor is it an ethnographic case study, a rich and careful description of a cultural setting. This story is a teaching case. It is a description of troubling and problematic events written to help prospective teachers think through the complex and ambiguous situations which arise in rural teaching. Teaching cases have long been a cornerstone of professional preparation in schools of business and law. Only recently has the field of education begun to explore their value in the preparation of teachers (Doyle, 1886; Shulman, 1987; McCarthy, 1987). In the teaching case, interpretations are left open and loose ends are not tied up. The teaching case demands speculation from inadequate knowledge. The purpose of the case is not to establish "truth" but rather to prepare students for "wise action" (Christensen, 1987). Professional practice demands wise action even where the truth neither is nor can be known.

Purposes of Teaching Cases

A teaching case presents a professional problem or dilemma and asks students to interpret the situation and decide upon a strategy for handling it. The case asks the student to figure out what is really going on, what went wrong, and what should be done.

Such cases provide vicarious experience, the opportunity to reflect upon common and complex dilemmas before actually encountering them. Teachers, like many other professionals, work in situations of great complexity, ambiguity, and disorder, where it is not clear what goals are desirable or where desirable goals conflict (Schon, 1983). In *Cross-Cultural Counseling*, as an example, the goal of increasing Yup'ik students' enrollment in college may conflict with the goal of maintaining a vital Yup'ik village community. Does the academically able young woman who chooses to stay home and baby-sit her sister's four children after high school represent a success or a failure of the school counseling program? What is the village high school supposed to be preparing Yup'ik students for?

Such dilemmas are at the heart of cross-cultural teaching. Deciding how to approach them requires far more than scientific generalizations or the pedagogical knowledge gained from methods courses. These dilemmas involve ethical issues, policy questions, interpersonal sensitivities, and political acumen, not only knowledge about alternative guidance techniques. Teaching cases are intended to show prospective teachers that such ethical and policy questions are inextricably interwoven in what may seem to be the ordinary and mundane activities of school life. Teaching cases give students practice in figuring out just what the problems are—what lawyers refer to as "issue spotting"—and how to frame these problems in fruitful ways.

Rural communities, even within the same cultural region, are different from each other and communities are changing in unpredictable ways. Different generations and different families within the same community do not have the same beliefs, expectations, values, and styles of communication. Teachers can expect no rules or recipes. They must learn how to learn from the specific situation.

A major purpose of teaching cases is to develop students' sensitivity to the situation—to the ambiguities and multiple realities of concrete experience. We want students to feel more comfortable with uncertainty. We want them to think about other people's interpretations of a situation. We want to enlarge their repertoire of potential strategies for accomplishing educational purposes. We want them to be better able to anticipate the ramifications and risks of the actions they may choose.

Teaching cases not only help to develop cognitive capacities—judgment and insight. The cases also offer emotional preparation for dealing with an unjust and uncertain world. Young teachers typically expect a just and orderly world, a world in which good teaching is always rewarded and good teachers do not bear the legacy of a past they did not create. Why should a generous and hard-working teacher like Fred Young, for example, face such hostility from a Yup'ik student like Myrna over what seems to be a question of whether or not he promised her a free soft drink for attending a guidance meeting? The cases help prospective teachers become aware that their expectations for a just world are not entirely reasonable and that people like themselves can become caught in circumstances not of their own making.

Representativeness of Cases and the Author's Point of View

Cross-Cultural Counseling is based on the author's experience as a teacher and site counselor in village high schools. Names and identifying details have been changed to protect confidentiality. The case is a composite which draws upon his experiences in several villages.

In preparing such cases, we have wrestled with the vexing issue of point of view. The author tells the story from the perspective of a teacher, and this story would be very different if told from a different perspective, such as the view of a student or community member. While the author tries to describe community perspectives, he is well aware that his viewpoint is limited. We all live within our own skins.

Students should discuss directly the limitations of the author's perspective and how the situation might look to others in the story. They should keep in mind that they too will have a limited view of events—the view of the teacher—and that they too will have to make decisions based upon a limited perspective and inadequate knowledge.

Studying and Teaching a Case

Teaching cases such as this one are intended to develop students' abilities to 1) spot issues and frame problems in an ambiguous and complex teaching situation, 2) interpret the situation from different perspectives, 3) identify different possibilities for action, and 4) consider the risks and ramifications of different courses of action.

In stimulating such reflection, we have found useful the following kinds of questions. Most have been culled from the instructor's guide to *Teaching and the Case Method* (Christensen, Hansen, & Moore, 1987) and from discussions about case method teaching (Christensen, 1987).

The questions are:

1. What are the central problems in this case? What is going wrong here? Is anything going wrong at all? From whose perspective?

2. What, if anything, should the teacher do differently next year? Why do you think so?

3. How does this situation appear to other participants such as the students? other teachers at the school? administrators in the central office? parents in the community?

4. How did this situation develop? What, if anything, might alter the basic conditions which created the present difficulties?

5. What, if anything, have you learned from this case?

In teaching a case, we typically ask students to prepare for class discussion by writing a two-page paper identifying what they see as the main issues in the case, describing the actions the teacher took, and appraising the teacher's actions. We begin the class by asking each student to identify the most important issues of the case and we list the issues on the chalkboard. We choose as a starting point for discussion an issue which many students have identified as key to understanding the case and an issue in which students are emotionally involved. The most memorable and powerful learning occurs where a case involves both the intellect and the emotions.

After the case discussion, we ask students to write another short paper on what they now see as the fundamental issues of the case, what actions they would have advised the teacher to take, and what they have learned or come to appreciate as a result of discussion and further reflection on the situation.

Issues Raised in Cross-Cultural Counseling: The Reluctant Seniors and the Guidance Project

As students read this case, it is helpful to keep two sets of problems in mind:

1) What adult lifestyles do students see as possibilities for themselves? What cultural shifts and conflicts have made the pathways to adulthood so undefined for Yup'ik students or are these pathways defined in ways that the teacher Fred Young does not see or appreciate?

2) What should Fred Young attempt to accomplish as site guidance counselor the following year? Which aspects of his previous approach worked well and why? What should he be trying to accomplish and what should count as a measure of success?

List of Characters

Fred Young	the site guidance counselor and a teacher at Tutuluq High School, a small rural high school in a Yup'ik community
Katie Young	Fred's wife and the special education teacher
Paul Best	principal, Tutuluq High School
Aaron Pete	Yup'ik high school teacher
Agnes Johnson	Yup'ik kindergarten teacher
Bertha Henderson	itinerant guidance counselor at Mountain and Valley School District
Mary, Eva, Adeline, Myrna	senior girls at Tutuluq High School
Jerry, Isaac, Nick, Nathan, Emil	senior boys at Tutuluq High School

Part I:
Background and Context

The Guidance Project

Ducking out of a raw January wind, Fred Young stopped at the darkened front entry of Tutuluq High School. The small brown frame building, set on pilings in the Arctic permafrost, stood at the edge of the tightly clustered Yup'ik homes. Fred took off one glove, reached into his down parka for his keys, unlocked the door, and hurried inside. As usual, at fifteen minutes to eight, he was the first teacher to arrive.

Fred walked down the short hallway past the still empty school office and unlocked his classroom door. Preoccupied with the senior guidance project which was to begin Monday morning, he hardly noticed the stacks of ungraded essays littering his desk. He had pinned his hopes on this guidance project, a way of actively involving his seniors in deciding what they would do the year after they graduated.

He paused, turned on the lights, and admired the work he had done to decorate his bulletin boards. **"WHAT DO YOU WANT TO DO?"** was the message in large letters cut out of red construction paper. Beneath, in white letters, was the message **"ONLY YOU CAN DECIDE."** And beneath, in yellow letters, read **"DON'T DO IT JUST FOR YOURSELF—DO IT FOR YOUR FUTURE—DO IT NOW."** The effect, he admitted to himself, was a bit corny, what with using the school colors and all, but it wasn't bad. Fred unloaded his knapsack and began to prepare for the day. He tried not to dwell on his anxieties about the project.

The senior guidance project was his last big effort to fulfill a goal he had set for himself at the beginning of the school year—motivating his seniors to do something the year following their graduation: attend a trade school, go to college, or even join the military. As the designated Site Guidance Counselor for Tutuluq High School, he had tried during the fall months to get the seniors interested in preparing for their future. But he had met with limited success. Now it was January—financial aid forms and college applications would soon be due. He hoped he had come up with something—a special two-week guidance project that would inspire his reluctant students. It was such a great idea! During these two weeks, students would look through catalogs to find the right schools for themselves. They would fill out forms and applications in his language arts class.

People from the village would come and speak to the seniors. Some would be Yup'ik elders who spoke little English and others would be younger people in charge of the Alaska Native village and regional corporations that made major business decisions. By the end of the two weeks, he hoped, every senior would have come up with a plan for the year after high school.

Fred was uneasy about the reception his project would receive from the administration. The counseling project was scheduled to use time during the seniors' regularly scheduled English class. How would his principal, Paul Best, react to such an unorthodox use of Fred's English teaching time? Wouldn't it be wiser just to stick to the course objectives outlined in the *Language Arts Curriculum Guide* set forth by the Mountain and Valley School District (MVSD)? Was it out of line to take time from English class when many students needed so much practice in using the English language? In all the in-service meetings he had attended, Fred heard one message over and over again: To improve the skills of the students of MVSD in all areas of the curriculum, it is essential first to improve their English language skills. Now he was about to start a project which would certainly use Yup'ik, the language of the community and the language of choice among his students, as much as English. Fred decided to let the principal in on his plans right away this morning. He knew he should have done so weeks ago.

Fred also worried about the village participants whom he had asked to come to school to describe their work: would they actually come? He had asked some villagers who were working for pay to give brief descriptions of their jobs. He had also asked some of the village elders who did not have a specific, paying job to talk to the students. Some of them might not be able to come because of specific conflicts. But he also knew that, in the Yup'ik culture, prearranging a time and place to visit was a foreign concept. People usually visited on a whim or, when meetings were called, they arrived near a certain time rather than exactly at a time. The silent message sent by those who did not show up might reinforce for his seniors the idea that preparing now for the future was not necessary. Would one of the elders actually come out and say what he had heard some of the students echo: "School is nothing"? School didn't prepare you for anything important and worthwhile. He wouldn't even know if the sentiment was expressed because he didn't speak Yup'ik.

What about the students who had already made decisions for their futures and were well on the way to completing their preparations? Would most of this two-week project be a waste of time for them? Was he emphasizing this project mostly to get those students who had resisted making a decision to give in and finally decide on something? Fred was troubled by his motives: was the real purpose of the project just to gratify his own ego?

On the other hand, the school's philosophy was to help students achieve a career. Fred felt he had not done enough as site guidance counselor to help the seniors. The more effort he put into his career guidance duties, the more he realized how little he really knew about the postgraduation needs of his Yup'ik seniors. Involving members of the village in the project, he hoped, would stimulate his reluctant seniors to take their futures into their own hands.

Fred Young and His Background

Fred Young had never thought of himself as someone qualified to counsel high-school students, let alone to counsel Yup'ik students. He was not new to living in an Eskimo village, but he was a relative newcomer to teaching.

Fred had graduated from a university in the Pacific Northwest with a double major in English and political science. He took a summer job in construction and later set up a business with a friend in the construction industry. One summer he took a business vacation to Alaska in order to construct a house in a Yup'ik village. He liked the immense vistas of unspoiled land and water and he liked the people he met. Fred decided to stay on in the village through the winter.

Because he was viewed as an expert in construction, Fred answered many requests to help the villagers learn the tricks of the trade. He taught all his skills many times over while helping one person do this and another do that. People repaid him by taking him out and introducing him to the ways of subsisting in the environment surrounding the village. Fred settled in and entered the cycle of life which dominated the village, a cycle set into motion by the seasonal changes. He also served as a substitute teacher at the village school.

One fall a new special education teacher, Katie, arrived in the village, and a mutual attraction developed between them. Fred decided to return to college to obtain a teaching certificate and Katie went with him to complete her master's degree. They looked forward to their return to Alaska and hoped they would be able to get jobs in the same village. When MVSD offered them contracts to teach in Tutuluq, they accepted the positions without reservations.

The Yup'ik Community of Tutuluq

Tutuluq, a village of about 500 people, is located on the bank of a river not too far from the Bering Sea. Its present location is the second place to be called by the name Tutuluq. The former village site, five miles further upriver, was originally a winter camp. The past lifestyle of the Yup'ik people was nomadic, moving from winter camp to summer camp as food sources fluctuated. The original winter site with its abandoned sod houses and small cemetery has become a living page of history for the new generation.

In the 1950s the Bureau of Indian Affairs decided to build an elementary school in Tutuluq. Because of danger from flooding, the villagers relocated to the present site. The village had no local high school until the late 1970s. Before that time, those students who wanted a high school education went away to boarding school, but many dropped out and returned home. In 1976, the Tobeluk vs. Lind settlement changed everything: all high school students won the right to receive an education in their home village. In Tutuluq the high school and grade school are now combined into one building. The high school has one large classroom, a half-size gym, a small shop area, a small kitchen, two bathrooms, a washroom, and an office.

High schools have become the very heart of most villages but their function is oddly unclear. What exactly are the schools preparing students for? The Yup'ik culture remains strong in Tutuluq. Yup'ik is still the language of choice. Grass is collected to construct baskets, and people use furbearing mammals to make parkas and ruffs. Trapping provides a source of cash income. Seals, fish, berries, and plants are essential to the diet. Traditional dances, potlatches, and subsistence activities remain an important part of life.

But Western influences are also strong. The Catholic church unites the village. Schools, grocery stores, and government offices dominate the landscape. A modern lighted runway allows planes to land, even on the darkest of winter days. The Alascom satellite dish links Tutuluq by television and telephone to the outside world.

Many students want to remain in Tutuluq, but the village does not have a self-sustaining cash economy. Few jobs are available in the community. The Army National Guard maintains a post in the village and employs twenty-one men and twelve women on a part-time basis. The Mountain and Valley School District employs about fifteen villagers as teacher aides, maintenance personnel, and cooks. Only two Yup'ik people are among the teaching and administrative staff. The city government employs four clerks and the village corporation, which operates a grocery store and a hardware store, has a manager and two or three cashiers on its payroll. There are only a few other wage-earning jobs—five air service agents, two operating engineers for the power plant, two store clerks, and a telephone repairman.

Men in the community earn cash in the winter by trapping fox, otter, and other furbearing animals whose skins they sell to furbuyers in the regional center, Salmonville. In summer, some of the men fish commercially for herring and salmon.

Everyone also participates in the subsistence economy by hunting waterfowl, seals, and caribou; fishing; drying game; rendering seal fat into oil; gathering and preserving edible vegetation; collecting grasses and preparing them for weaving baskets; and saving driftwood for winter use as a fuel.

Part II:
Reluctant Seniors

Fred Young as Site Guidance Counselor

At the first staff meeting during his second year in Tutuluq, Fred found himself the new guidance counselor. The teacher who had previously been the guidance counselor had left unexpectedly.

"So what exactly does the site counselor have to do?" Katie asked him that evening.

"Well, I'm not sure, but I guess the first thing I'm going to concentrate on is getting the seniors involved in making some sort of career decisions. I hope I can bring a little excitement into the concept of choosing a career."

"You'll bring a lot of excitement, honey. Are you going to have time to do it?"

"I should. I really don't think it should be that time consuming to give the seniors an insight into options open to them. It will just take a little planning."

"Just remember to take some time for yourself this year. Last year you were overwhelmed. You promised you would get out to the tundra more."

"I know, I know. I will. But someone has to do this. The seniors need so much direction. I'm going to get them all thinking right now about what they want to do next fall. And then, they're all going to commit to something and do it!"

Fred made up a year-long schedule for getting together with the seniors. Because he didn't have time to deal with counseling duties formally on a daily basis, he scheduled an after-school meeting on the second Tuesday of each month as official guidance time.

By the first guidance meeting, Fred had already spent about ten hours in guidance activities and yet had hardly given any advice to the seniors. He had mentioned to his seniors that they should begin thinking about what they wanted to do after they graduated, but he had given them no suggestions on next steps. Mary Sipary, one of the seniors, had come to him with a scholarship application for the National Guard, which he had helped her begin to fill out, but she was the only one who had come to him for help.

Fred had been spending all his spare time redoing the modest counseling center which the past guidance counselor had used the previous year. He discarded old college catalogs and replaced them with new ones which had accumulated over the summer. Each school day brought more mail addressed to "Counselor, Tutuluq High School" which had to be dealt with. Fred stuck the mail in a holding box in the counseling center until he had time to put it away properly.

The center had a drawer for each of the post-high-school choices most popular with past seniors. As he became familiar with the center, Fred began to understand that he had jumped into a position which he had very little idea how to go about filling. The amount of information in the center was vast. He also began to realize that someone had already put a great deal of effort into organizing the center. Maybe last year's guidance counselor had done more than he thought. He remembered his distinct feeling last year that this person had not worked too hard at guidance counseling. Had he been mistaken?

Fred saw the drawer labeled *Financial Aid* as the heart of the center. Not one senior could rely completely on the financial resources of his or her family to attend college or trade school. The *Financial Aid* drawer was chaotic. There were scholarship forms mixed with loan forms mixed with *Financial Aid Forms* and announcements of contests for scholarships. Pamphlets like *101 Places to Find Financial Aid* were buried with pamphlets like *Where to Find Hidden Money for College*. When would he have time to read them? If he didn't read them, how would he understand all the potential resources available for his seniors? The amount of time he was going to have to put into counseling was going to be a whole lot more than the sixteen hours he had originally estimated for the principal Paul Best and submitted on the required extra-pay-for-extra-duty form. The money didn't bother Fred. He had become familiar with expectations for teachers in the villages. But it did bother him that he might not have enough time to do as good a job as he had hoped. Would he be able to get each of the seniors ready for their lives after high school? Where should he start?

The second guidance session, he decided, would focus on financial aid. By then he would have a better idea of how the seniors should begin to apply for it. At the moment, his concepts of financial aid were about as organized as the contents of the counseling center.

Fred announced to his senior English class the time and date of the first counseling session a week before it was to be held. "It's going to be an important get-together for seniors only," he said. He put up posters with the slogan, *Seniors, Bring Your Dreams to Life,* as a memory booster. He promised free soft drinks to all who attended. A couple of students complained that they had cross-country practice, but the promise of a soft drink at least got them to the beginning of the meeting.

As the seniors arrived, Fred handed each one a soda and asked that they browse through the bookshelves and drawers in the counseling center. Most of the seniors were willing to look at the catalogs and information. Fred was gratified by their comments.

"Wow, look at this."

"Gee, I wonder what it's like at this place?"

"So deadly!"

"Where's the UAF catalog?"

"I want to go to ROTC."

"Construction, man, construction. I want to make lots of money."

"No way! Pilots make the money."

"I can't find anything in here about the Marines."

When Jerry Olinka, a senior boy, arrived and asked, "What are you guys doing?" Fred decided to get the students together.

"Okay, seniors!" Fred said, raising his voice to be heard. "Let's call the session to order."

It made him feel good to see the seniors smiling and for the most part enthusiastic to hear what he had to say. He wanted to keep it that way throughout the year. His hope was to develop camaraderie among the seniors so that they might inspire each other into developing plans.

"Here's the deal," Fred said, opening the meeting. "Next year at this time not one of you is going to be here. You'll be graduated!"

"All right."

"Yahoo."

"No more teachers' dirty looks!"

"I know it sounds crazy, but you have to start planning now. Right now you need to plan this year for what you'll be doing next year. If you want to go to college, now is the time to decide where to go. If you want to go to a vocational school, now is the time. It's not easy making decisions about which dreams you want to come true, so I want all of us to work together. By May, when you all have your caps and gowns on, you will know where you are going!"

Fred handed out the schedules and explained that it was the seniors' responsibility to meet on every second Tuesday for the rest of the year to share information and work together.

"Use this counseling center any time to help you decide what you want to do and where you want to go. Read about the colleges. Read about the National Guard, the Navy, the Marines, the Army. Read about vocational schools! But get ready now to make your dreams come true. Who's got questions?"

"Can we go now?"

"No, you can't go now. We still have half an hour left. Now what I want everyone to do is take one of these drawers and sort through the information. Throw everything that has a date on it before last year into a big pile here for the trash."

By the end of the afternoon, some of the drawers had been thinned out, but the bulk of them were untouched. The seniors' efforts had helped, but their enthusiasm had begun to wane with the last of the soft drinks. When they had gone to cross-country practice or home to do chores, Fred had stayed and continued cleaning out drawers and organizing materials somewhat obsessively, knowing that he was neglecting his responsibilities of preparing for his next day's lessons.

Fred had come to realize that sometimes it was necessary to let classes slide. What he had better do as soon as possible was make certain that each of the seniors would have enough credits to graduate. He wanted to be very, very sure. In another village one of the seniors thought he was going to graduate only to find out two weeks before graduation that he did not have enough credits. On the day before graduation he committed suicide. The family blamed the school.

Nine seniors had attended the meeting, five boys and four girls. Of the five boys, Fred was certain that Jerry Olinka had no hope of graduating this year and thought that two others might not have the credits to graduate either. Fred didn't feel he should exclude them or point out in front of their peers the fact that they did not have the credits to graduate the coming spring. He considered them "nonsenior" seniors.

Jerry was nineteen, the oldest student in the high school. This was Jerry's second year of nonsenior status. Fred had been impressed last year by Jerry's love of writing. His syntax was poor, but it was evident that he put a lot of thought into his work. Jerry fell quickly behind in other work, but his journal was always complete and full of insights into the Yup'ik perspective. Invariably, Jerry's journal contained the phrase ". . . in the old days . . ."

Fred had been surprised to see Jerry back again on the first day of school. Last year Jerry had transferred to a neighboring village, just before the end of the fall semester. Jerry had missed a lot of school before he left. Because he failed to register in his new high school until the spring semester, he received no credit for any of his fall classes. Fred did not know why he had left, although he had heard rumors that another student had beaten up and threatened Jerry. Whatever his reason for leaving, Fred had welcomed Jerry back and asked him how he had done.

"Fine, but they didn't like me down there."

Getting nothing more out of Jerry, Fred decided to call and ask that Jerry's transcript be sent. While talking to the principal, Fred learned that Jerry had earned no credits for any class. When Fred asked for elaboration, the principal gave the phone to one of the teachers, explaining that he knew nothing about Jerry's performance because he had just transferred to this school from another village. The teacher who came on the line was brief and to the point. "Jerry was a very poor student. He was consistently late to class. He did no homework. Finally, he just stopped coming to class at all. He would have gotten an F in my class if he had kept coming."

Fred thanked the teacher, asked that a transcript be forwarded, and hung up. Jerry had gone to school for the better part of a year and come away with absolutely nothing, except perhaps some bitterness about school and what it stood for.

Fred thought about what he should do for Jerry. So far he wasn't getting anywhere. During the first week of school, Fred had approached Jerry when he was alone, and asked him about his spring semester.

Jerry was concentrating on a computer game and kept his eyes on the screen. "Those teachers down there, I don't think they liked me."

"Why do you say that?" Fred asked, taking a seat by Jerry.

"I guess they all flunked me."

"Did you go to school?"

"Yeah, I went to school."

"Every day?"

"Yeah, I guess so. I can't remember."

"Well, here's the deal, Jerry. I called down there to get your transcript sent up and they told me you didn't get credit in any of your classes."

Jerry looked over to Fred. "Not any of 'em?"

"No. None. Did you think you passed any?"

"Yes. No. Well, I don't know," Jerry said, concentrating on the computer. It was obvious that Jerry was uncomfortable with the direct confrontation.

"Well, until the transcript gets here, I'm going to assume that you didn't pass any, like the principal there told me."

"Yeah. Okay."

"Do you know what you're going to have to do now?"

"Take 'em over?"

"Right. Do you know what your biggest problem is about school?"

"No one gets me to school? I don't know."

"No. Do you think all the students depend on their parents to get them up in the mornings?"

"Maybe."

"It's got to be you, Jerry. Do you know how you are going to make sure you pass all your classes this year?"

Jerry looked up again, eager to hear. "How?"

"By getting to every class, every day, on time."

Jerry's smile faded and he turned back to the computer. "I'll try."

"I want to help you get your credits this year, Jerry, so if anything or anyone is bothering you, please feel free to tell me. You are going to have a successful year."

Fred stood up and put his hand on Jerry's shoulder. "Right, Jerry?"

"I'll try."

Fred decided that Jerry hadn't received his advice very well. Had he been too direct with Jerry? Had everyone else lectured him so often he no longer listened? What had Jerry been trying to say about his parents? Could it be so simple that the kid just needed some love?

Fred packed up and left for home. He was far from feeling the first guidance session had been a success when Katie asked him how the session had gone.

"Did many of the seniors come?"

"Oh, yeah. Nine seniors, 100 percent attendance. The advertising worked, especially with the free pop thrown in. I had to tell some of the juniors to come back next year."

"Sounds like a success."

"From that standpoint, it was. But when the pop ran out so did their enthusiasm. Oh, I don't mean to be so cynical. A few were genuinely interested in doing something next year. Isaac is really gung-ho on aviation school or the National Guard. The Guard was the most popular."

"Well, honey, you can't blame them. After all, it is one of the most prevalent role models in the village. The fact is, the National Guard carries a lot of prestige in all the villages out here. You know that."

"I know, but I really want them to open their eyes to some of the other opportunities available. I just can't bear the thought of someone like Mary going into the military."

"She wants to be in the Guard? That would be a waste. She's got to go to college."

"Well, I'm going to try to convince her, believe me."

"What about Nathan? What does he think he might do?"

"Nothing."

"Is he thinking of a vocational school?"

"No."

"College? Well, he's not really college material."

18 • Cross-Cultural Counseling

"No, he's thinking of nothing. He said he couldn't wait until next year so he could get up in the morning and have nothing to do!"

Katie laughed. "What a nut! Well, it's inevitable that some of them are going to stay right here in Tutuluq after they graduate."

"I know. I know it is. But I'm going to give them every opportunity to see what there is to do if they do decide to leave. It's not like those who leave never come back. Even the ones who go to college eventually come back here."

"Not all of them."

"Well, I'd say most of them, at least the ones who don't marry into another village. Look at Aaron Pete. He's a perfect example. He went to college for two years, then came back here and got a job as an aide with the high school and did some correspondence study. Then he went through the rural teacher's program at UAF. And now he's teaching at the high school."

"Well, Nathan isn't exactly the same as Aaron."

"I wasn't trying to say he was. All I was trying to say was that it seems to me most of the villagers who leave to go back to school for training or boot camp usually find their way back here. So that's why I am going to encourage all the seniors to line up something to do for next fall. I don't want to see them just do nothing."

"Oh, Fred, I think Nathan was just kidding when he told you that he was going to do nothing next year. When Nathan talks about looking forward to doing nothing, I think he means nothing that isn't subsistence lifestyle, and that's a lot of work."

"It's a beautiful way of life which we are changing," Fred replied, his ambivalence showing through.

"Sure it is. But for goodness' sake, we're out here giving them new skills to function in the modern world. And you're getting them ready to go to college or trade school or whatever it is that they're going to do," Katie insisted.

"What is it we're trying to prepare the students for by the time they're ready to graduate, anyhow?" Fred asked her the question he had worried about many times.

"To function as active participants in their world," she said. "It's no different here than it is in Anchorage or Seattle or Anywhere, USA."

"No, it's not the same at all. Which world are we preparing them for? The traditional or the modern?"

"Which do you think?"

The Itinerant Counselor from Mountain and Valley School District

Bertha Henderson, the itinerant guidance counselor, was scheduled for a visit early in the fall. Bertha was based in the central office. She organized the district's guidance activities and occasionally visited each school. Her reputation as a less-than-engrossing presenter reached Fred early. One morning, one of the students came up and asked Fred, "Do we have to sit and listen to old boring Bertha tomorrow?" Fred asked the student to fill him in.

That afternoon Fred took the opportunity to meet Bertha when she arrived in the village. She had come to "give them a little career guidance and have them take the Armed Services Vocational Aptitude Battery... you know, that's for the ones who are interested in the military. And of course I'll be giving the ACT test; that is for the ones who are interested in getting into college."

Bertha may have had the interests of the students at heart. But, sitting in the back of the class and listening to her presentation, Fred understood all too well why she was known as "boring Bertha." Her films were irrelevant to the lifestyle of the students. Her monotone manner all but lulled the class to sleep. Bertha plugged along, oblivious to the fact that not one student was following one word she said. Fred was dismayed. The students, it seemed, associated the whole notion of careers with absolute and complete boredom.

Fred had tried to put some life into the counseling program earlier in the year. He had called Bertha and asked her for advice on what he could do. She had reassured him. "You're already doing all you can by getting me out there on my first stop! I'll be glad to sit down with you and answer any questions you have. Oh, wait a minute, Fred, there is something. Are you going to be sending any of your seniors on the bus trip?"

"Bus trip? What's that?"

"I take it you haven't received the information. You should have it by now. It's a trip we've organized for the seniors who are interested in going to college or vocational school. We'll start in Anchorage where we've rented a bus. We'll look at the University of Alaska Anchorage and the Alaska Business College and then go over to the university in Fairbanks and, we hope, get the kids down to Seward to the vocational center. It should be a whale of a trip, and I think there's still space if you're interested."

"I'm interested! Is it on the district or does it come out of our site budget?"

"Oh, I wish the district could. No, it comes out of the site budgets and it's $600 per student. It should be a real good trip though."

"Okay. Sounds great. I'll talk to the principal and see if we have any money. Thanks, Bertha."

Fred approached Paul Best about the trip, but came away empty-handed. There was no money in the budget for the activity. It would have meant canceling a basketball trip. Besides, according to the principal, the Tutuluq Advisory School Board had established a policy on student travel: Money spent on group activities is preferred to money spent on individual student activities. Fred argued a bit for sending some of the more motivated seniors, but to no avail.

Last Year's Seniors

Fred worried about his guidance responsibilities. What was the district policy toward seniors? Were they forgotten once graduated? Had any studies shown what sorts of things held the greatest promise of success for Yup'ik students after high school? Why was it that so many of the young men seemed less apt to go to college and, once there, less apt to succeed? What could be done to get them more involved in pursuing an education or a career after high school? How strong an influence should he try to be in deciding the future of the students?

Fred thought about his seniors from last year. Of them, two young men and a young woman had gone into the National Guard and were looking forward to going into boot camp at the start of the new year. In Fred's opinion, the young woman, Charlene, and one of the young men should have gone to college.

One afternoon on his way to the store, Fred had seen Charlene coming toward him on the boardwalk. She was babysitting her sister's children, two in a wagon behind her, one pushing the wagon, and the last holding her free hand. He stopped to find out what she had done over the summer and what she would be doing in the coming months. She looked down at the boardwalk as they approached each other.

"Hi, Charl, how was your summer?" Fred asked.

Charlene looked up smiling. "Is that Fred?"

"Sure, it's me. Don't you even recognize your most favorite teacher?"

Charlene laughed. "You look funny, different. I thought you were some stranger," she said, shaking her head. "Did you shave your beard?"

"No," Fred replied, "I don't know what happened. It just fell off one night."

"Naaaa, youuuu," Charlene laughed, looking up. "You shaved."

"I did, you're right," Fred confessed. "I finally took your advice. It looks good, though, doesn't it?"

"No," Charlene laughed, "it looks funny! Your *magojik* looks ugly!" Charlene gestured to her own chin to indicate what she meant by *magojik*.

Fred laughed back, "Thanks a lot!"

"So when are you leaving for college?" he asked.

"I'm not going to college."

"What do you mean you're not going to college?" Fred asked, amazed.

"I don't know. I guess I decided not to go."

"Why not?"

"Fairbanks is too far. My family didn't want me to be so far away."

"Well, what about Salmonville Community College?" Fred asked. "It's close. It would be perfect."

"I don't want to go. Oh gosh, my English skills aren't good enough. My sister told me I wouldn't do very well 'cause my English is baaad!"

"No way, Charlene! Your English is great." Fred couldn't believe what he was hearing. Charlene had the strongest English skills of last year's seniors. "You would do just fine in college. It's not that much different from high school. You should go!"

"I can't even read a book. I didn't read a book all summer."

"So what? That doesn't mean you can't read. You should try SCC. It's not too late to apply. You're a good student!"

"Naaaa, I'm gonna go National Guard. Basic training is in January."

Fred knew her mind was made up. He was amazed that Charlene had opted against college. It bothered him that she felt her English skills weren't good enough. Hadn't he given her any confidence in her own abilities? Had she really not read a book all summer? Probably not. She probably hadn't spoken English more than a few times all summer either. After all, there was little need to. He should have given her some books to read over the summer. It sounded as though her older sister had influenced her decision.

Fred caught himself. He shouldn't be disappointed that Charlene was only babysitting for her sister. He knew strong family bonds had played a large part in the survival of the Yup'ik culture for thousands of years in extremely hostile conditions. What business did he have in trying to influence her? Why should he feel bad that Charlene had chosen the military over college? At least she was doing something! It was her decision. Still he knew that if he had been the guidance counselor last year, he would have seen to it that she was on her way to college.

Two other seniors—Bernice, the valedictorian, and Sam, the salutatorian of last year's class—had chosen to go to the University of Alaska in Fairbanks. Bernice had been the most motivated student that Fred had ever known. She did meticulous work, making sure she received A grades in all of her classes. She had been the student council president. To Fred, she epitomized the modern Yup'ik student—skilled in traditional crafts and respectful of traditional customs while at the same time adept in all of her classes.

Fred had been surprised the previous year when Bernice had come to him and asked if she should apply to Harvard. She explained that she was asking all the teachers to give her their opinions for "secret" reasons. Fred had urged her to apply. He thought it reasonable to assume that, with her grades and her minority background, she might be accepted, and he told her this. Later, when Bernice was talking with him, he found out that she indeed had been accepted into Harvard. Fred found out that another teacher had urged Bernice to go instead to the University of Alaska Fairbanks because of its extensive support systems for Native students. In Fred's mind, this was a mistake.

Fred had, however, been very excited that Sam would attend UAF. Sam had talked about it all year. Although Fred and the other staff suspected that Sam abused drugs, this drug use had not interfered with his performance in school. He had maintained his excellent class standing.

During the second guidance session in October, Fred mentioned Sam's name as someone who would be in Fairbanks to help those who went to college to find their way around. One of the seniors informed Fred that Sam had never gone to Fairbanks at all. Sam had been in Salmonville during registration and had missed the deadline. Now he was still in Tutuluq "partying hard."

The District In-Service Meeting on Guidance

As the site counselor, Fred was required to go to a ninety-minute session specifically on the subject of counseling at the district in-service which was held in late October. Bertha Henderson handed the site guidance counselors the MVSD handbook, which spelled out the district's counseling goals: "To provide comprehensive career and vocational counseling services including individual analysis, information dissemination, personal counseling and interpretation, placement services, and follow-up services."

Two representatives from the nonprofit department of the Asiqtuq Regional Native Corporation spoke about financial aid. Both the president of Salmonville Community College and a recent graduate of SCC talked about the community college program.

From the first Asiqtuq Corporation speaker, Fred learned that each student who was accepted into a college could receive a $1,000 scholarship per semester from Asiqtuq Corporation. First, students had to file the *Financial Aid Form* (FAF). The FAF is four pages long and requires that the student and the student's parents disclose all income that they received and reported to the IRS on their most recent income tax filing. The speaker was blunt about the fact that many students who thought that they were going to receive monies for college did not receive them because the form was filled out incorrectly or submitted after the deadline. It was imperative that counselors insure that the forms were turned in on time and filled out correctly. Further, it often was a difficult job to get the parents to disclose their income for a number of reasons. Sometimes they were simply unwilling to let people know how much money they made and sometimes they did not file income tax forms. Only if students could prove they were not claimed as dependents of their parents, could they receive money without an income tax form.

This speaker also clarified for Fred the differences between loans, scholarships, and grants. Loans are available to the students through the Alaska Student Loan Program. The danger is that many students do not realize that they are required to pay these back after they have been out of school for more than twelve months.

Cross-Cultural Counseling • 25

The speaker advised that students not be encouraged to take these loans out. A typical pattern for rural students is to go to college for a semester or two and then stop, never to go back, or to do so only a few years later. Then they are saddled with paying the loan back when, more likely than not, they have returned to their village and cannot get a job.

Scholarship money is available to the students based on merit. The money never has to be paid back. Grant money may be available for students who meet certain economic or social criteria. Repayment of grants sometimes entails service.

The second Asiqtuq Corporation speaker talked about students who wanted to go to technical school. Money is available through Job Training Program Assistance (JTPA). JTPA provides scholarship money to cover both the costs of the program and the costs of transportation, but there is a catch. The individual enrolled in the program has to have written proof of employment with an existing business upon graduation. In other words, the student has to have a job before he or she is eligible for a scholarship.

The Salmonville Community College president impressed on the site counselors that they should not overlook SCC as a potential choice for those students who were interested in going to college. The college granted associate degrees and most of the students then went on to get bachelor's degrees in Fairbanks. Because Salmonville was the hub for the Mountain and Valley area, he pointed out, the college was specifically attuned to the needs of the region's students. Finally, the president talked about SCC's mission to enroll young men. The college wanted to boost the numbers of young men, who were outnumbered two to one by young women.

The last speaker was a student who praised what SCC had done for her. The college, she said, had given her the confidence that she could succeed. She was especially thankful for the many hours after class which her teachers had spent working with her on her English skills. Fred was impressed with her. He knew from working with his students preparing for the MVSD speech tournament how difficult it must have been for her to get up in front of a crowd.

At lunch, Fred along with Barb Glass, a language arts teacher who was another site counselor, cornered Bertha and sat down with her.

"So how do you suggest I get some of my reluctant seniors interested in doing something after they graduate?" Fred asked.

"The truth is," Bertha replied, "they have to get themselves interested. If they aren't interested, they aren't going to make any effort to do the best they could."

"Well, isn't part of our job to get them interested?"

"Oh, yes. Definitely. But you can't push it down their throats. If you do, it'll come back to haunt you. Say you talk your seniors into going to college, and the students get there and find out that college isn't what they thought it would be. What do you think they are going to do?"

"They're going to be mad," Barb said. "I've had it happen. I had a student who wasn't sure whether she wanted to go to college and I convinced her to pursue it. I went so far as to write the letters for her to get the admissions package and filled out her FAF and she went off to Fairbanks. She was back in a month. She still won't speak to me about it."

"You're kidding," Fred said, disbelieving.

"No. I wish I was. She was one of my favorite students and the experience soured everything."

"Now you can't blame yourself, Barb," Bertha said. "We're only trying to help these kids. But if you push them into something they find out they don't want to be into, they'll be bitter. They'll blame you and they won't ever go back. And they'll take a long time to get over it."

"Well, some of my seniors are unsure about what they want to do. I've tried to get them to write some letters to get some information, but they want to wait until they are more sure," Fred said.

"But at the same time you have to push them just enough," Barb pointed out. "I have a student now who is attending the University of Frankfurt! He is doing marvelously. It is beyond my wildest imagination that James would be doing this."

Cross-Cultural Counseling • 27

"What? You have a student going to school in Germany? Do you offer German at your site?"

"No. Of course not. He didn't know a word of German until he got over there. It just blows me away to think of this Yup'ik- and English-speaking student over there holding his own in a German university."

"How did you do that?"

"It was something that he was interested in. He was the one who started it and I just kept giving him positive feedback and helped him pursue it. He's an excellent student, and he got a lot of support from his parents. I don't think James would have gone if he hadn't gotten that support, but then his parents have a broad perspective."

"That is so great! He's paving the way." Fred felt jealous.

"Well, I don't know about that, but maybe. Who knows?"

"I'm going to agree with you, Barb," Bertha said. "You do have to push a little bit. You have to keep on them to get those FAF forms in on time and to get their admission papers in on time. You have to be sure they meet the deadlines. Because, here again, if they don't get accepted because the papers were late, they're going to want to blame someone!"

Fred nodded his head.

"It's not easy, Fred," Bertha said, laughing. "Is it, Barb?"

"No. And you know some parents aren't going to want to send their children off either. Some of them are afraid they'll never see their children again if they go out of the village. You can't blame them, but . . ."

"I can see that I might have that problem," Fred interrupted. He was thinking of Isaac, one of his seniors. "Some of the parents depend on their children to keep the house running. Especially with things like hauling water and pumping fuel. And probably hunting, too."

28 • Cross-Cultural Counseling

"Exactly," Barb said, "and the sad thing is that the ones who would really do well outside the village are also the ones who shoulder the responsibilities. They'll stay home and help out and just sort of, you know, waste away."

"It's the ones who aren't really ready for college who end up going. So many drop out when they can't hack it and then end up on Fourth Avenue in Anchorage," Bertha added.

"So do you have any theory as to how to motivate the guys?" Fred asked. "It seems like I just can't get them into anything."

"That's the golden question. It seems as though they take a little longer to mature. Lots of times they just like to hang around the village and go hunting and chase the girls. Then after a few years they get bored and then start to think about the alternatives. Then some of them do go to college or a vocational school or come into Salmonville and find a job. Any insights, Barb?"

"No. Not really. It seems to me students will get involved in correspondence education if they understand what the course is and if they find out about it and if there is a SCC liaison in the village. A lot of it depends on the liaison also. The one in my village is incredible. No one was coming to the classes so she went and worked with the students in their homes."

"Wow! Talk about dedicated!

Upon his return to Tutuluq, Fred decided to lighten up a bit, but this mood didn't last long. Not all the seniors attended the second counseling session. Fred implored them to come to the next meeting. After all, they had some important decisions to make about their future.

The Third Guidance Session

The third guidance meeting was a fiasco. Basketball season was underway and practices had been scheduled for the boys right after school and for the girls at 7 P.M. Fred, therefore, scheduled a guidance session for the boys in the evening and for the girls right after school. Attendance for the girls was poor. Only two of the four girls showed up—Mary and Eva. They worked on finishing letters to the schools in which they were interested. Fred teased them about being so slow in completing them. "You've been working on them for two months now!"

Fred showed them how to use the computer to write the letters more easily. All that was necessary was to compose the letter once, and then change the name at the top of the letter to fit the school. He wished he had thought of it earlier. He made a mental note to let the students use English time to compose the letters. Fred had begun to worry about deadlines. Before the girls left, he gave them each a scholarship application to take home and fill out.

Just as Fred was getting ready to leave, Adeline and Myrna came in and asked if it was too late for the meeting. Adeline claimed she had been baby-sitting. Fred wanted to stay and work with them. They had shown so little interest so far that he had begun to wonder if they were going to do anything or not. Both were good students, although Myrna always seemed to be angry with a chip on her shoulder. Both girls were from more traditional families. Did they have role models? How little he really knew about his students. The thing which dismayed him was that he knew both of the girls had the potential to succeed in college. He recalled the young Yup'ik woman from the in-service. She could have easily been either of these girls. Why wasn't he able to get through to them? Fred wondered how he could influence their families to nudge them towards college. Would it be too pushy to make home visits?

Fred was tired. He told the girls they had missed the meeting but they were welcome to come that evening when he was going to meet with the boys.

When the girls reminded him that they had basketball practice, he gently but firmly told them that they had known about the meeting and, if it was important to them, they would miss basketball to come that evening. Otherwise they could come to talk to him after school any afternoon.

Of the five senior boys, only Isaac Steve and Jerry Olinka came. Fred handed them a pop as they arrived. Isaac claimed to have finished a letter to UAF, but had misplaced it. Fred believed him. One of his students' biggest problems was organization. No one had shown them how to be organized. Fred put Isaac to work on the computer getting his master letter composed.

Jerry had come to see if he could play computer games. He hadn't come to class that day, and Fred told him there was no way he could play a computer game. Instead, he let him use the computer to make a journal entry.

Fred was disheartened that Nick and Emil and Nathan hadn't come. Was he spending all his time spinning his wheels? What was it going to take to get these others involved?

Adeline and Myrna opted for basketball practice, and he wasn't surprised. But when they came into the classroom for a drink of water, Myrna dealt him one of those blows that he had come to know as a high-school teacher but which he would never get used to.

Fred said "Hi" to the girls as they walked in, but they turned away, unwilling to reciprocate the greeting. As they stopped behind Isaac and Jerry, Myrna said, in perfect English, "Don't believe anything that Fred*aaq* tells you. He lied to us big time today about getting a soda if we came to the meeting. College is for nothing anyhow."

Jerry replied, "Yeah, I know. That's what the old people say. School is for nothing."

Fred shouldn't have let it get to him, but it did.

The Staff Meeting

The principal, Paul Best, agreed to put Fred and the counseling program at the bottom of the agenda for the staff meeting, which fell on the following Tuesday. By the time Fred had the floor, it was late in a long day. Most of the classified personnel, who lived in the community, were gone because they were not required to stay after the close of the school day.

Fred had written up a list of questions:

1. What are we preparing our students for upon completion of high school?

2. Should we encourage our graduates to remain in the village or to pursue choices outside the village?

3. How can we best encourage the seniors to involve themselves in their futures?

4. What is the best way to keep Yup'ik traditions alive in our students?

He had hoped for a vigorous discussion. Looking around at the tired faces and stained coffee cups, he was dubious. But he plunged on.

"As you know, I'm the site guidance counselor this year," Fred began. "I've been working on some projects, but the students' interest has not been what I'd hoped. It occurred to me that there are some more basic questions in this guidance area that need to get sorted out. . . . I know it's late but maybe I could raise these questions with you.

"Here's my first question: 'What are we preparing our students for upon completion of high school?'"

People shifted in their seats. Finally one of the high school teachers said aggressively. "I think we should be preparing our students in vocational skills that they can use in the village if they decide not to leave the village."

Fred wondered if this comment was a reproach. Everyone knew how much he hoped kids would go on to college.

The primary grades teacher added, "We should prepare the students to be successful in any endeavor which they undertake."

No one said anything more. Fred decided to move on to his next question. "Should we encourage our graduates to remain in the village or to pursue choices outside the village?"

"Not all the students should be encouraged to attend college," said Aaron Pete, one of the Native teachers.

Fred looked up, a worried expression forming on his face.

"We should guide the students according to their own inclinations and according to their family's desires and wishes," said Paul Best, sensing tension.

"The military is okay but college or a vocational school would be better if they are interested," Aaron Pete continued.

Fred's anxiety eased. Maybe he had misinterpreted Aaron Pete's first remark. Maybe all Aaron was saying was that students shouldn't be pressured into college.

"Some of them shouldn't leave the village," commented Agnes Johnson, the other Native teacher at the school who taught kindergarten.

The meeting grew silent again.

Fred decided to go to his next question. Maybe he could get some specific ideas that would help him put together a guidance project. "How can we best encourage the seniors to involve themselves in their futures?"

"Find out what they are interested in," Agnes Johnson said.

"Have some role models come in and speak to them," suggested one of the high school teachers.

"The family is responsible for getting their senior involved," Agnes added.

"I'd say it should be one-fourth the senior, one-fourth the family, one-fourth the school, and one-fourth the community," said Aaron Pete.

No one said anything more. Fred sensed an uneasiness, although he couldn't figure out exactly what it was. The discussion wasn't going anywhere. Was there a conflict that people didn't want to bring out into the open? Or was everyone just tired and worn-out? Or maybe they had all been over this ground too many times before. Fred wondered if he was acting too much the bright-eyed and bushy-tailed new teacher.

"What is the best way to keep Yup'ik traditions alive in our students?" asked Fred, moving to his final question.

"Parents need to enforce traditional values at home by involving the students in traditional activities," said Agnes Johnson. She had made this point at faculty meetings many times before.

"In the school the best we can do is to convey at attitude which allows for a sense of pride in our heritage," said Aaron Pete. "Keeping traditions alive should be left to the individual."

Were Agnes Johnson and Aaron Pete in agreement, Fred wondered, or were they disagreeing? He tuned back into the discussion.

"We should invite the elders in to speak on a more regular basis and have them speak about values," said of the high school teachers, glancing at Agnes and Aaron.

The teachers fell silent once again. Paul Best thanked everyone for staying so late and people started to get up.

Fred felt better—especially after hearing Aaron Pete's view that getting students involved in their future was a responsibility equally shared by the students, the school, the family, and the community. But he didn't have any better angle on just what he should do about his guidance project.

By Christmas break, Mary, Eva, Isaac, and Emil had all written letters to colleges. Emil had been a surprise, but Fred had told the seniors that he would give extra credit in English for any letters of inquiry they turned in. Fred was beginning to worry about Emil because his attendance was dropping off. In the fall, Fred had made a home visit (with Aaron Pete as translator) to speak with the boy's grandfather. His mother had been out of the village for most of the fall. Emil had missed several days of school due to the hunting trips that he liked so much; he was starting to get dangerously close to receiving no credit in some of his classes. Adeline, Myrna, Nick, and Nathan had yet to show much interest in making plans.

Part III:
The Guidance Project

January Arrives and the Guidance Project Begins

When Fred arrived at school that raw January day, his new approach to senior guidance was in place. What remained a serious worry was how it would turn out. He reminded himself again to tell the principal about it right away. During the Christmas break, Fred's plan took shape. He would move guidance into his regular classroom time for a two-week intensive session. He thought about the comments made at the staff meeting about role models and having elders come in. He would definitely involve the community.

Back in the village after the break, Fred began to work on the senior guidance project he had envisioned. He gathered together all the books on occupations from the library and put them in his classroom. He asked villagers if they would be willing to come in for the seniors' sakes. The first thing on the agenda for the two-week session was to fill out the *Financial Aid Form*. Fred rationalized that this would be a motivator. After scanning the form, Fred realized none of the seniors would be able to fill one out by themselves. The vocabulary was too complex and the students might not have the necessary information. The seniors would also fill out the Asiqtuq Corporation forms. He had allotted Monday and Tuesday and part of Wednesday for these purposes.

On Wednesday he planned to give the students the complete set of volumes for the Alaska Career Information System (AKCIS), which was published by the Alaska Department of Education. He had placed the set in the counseling center early in the year. His advice to the seniors to use them had gone largely unheeded. AKCIS consisted of five volumes: *School Information*, *Occupational Information*, *Programs of Study and Training*, *Military Career Information*, and *Learning Activities and Implementation*. All the volumes were cross-referenced so that when the students found a job they were interested in they could find out where to get the schooling. Included with AKCIS was a computer disk with which the students could find jobs most suited to their interests. Fred thought that the students would enjoy the computer program. The next step was writing the master inquiry letter. They could finish by Friday. However, on Friday, the first of the speakers, Rudy Beluga, the president of the Tutuluq Associated School Board, was due to come speak to the seniors.

Thinking about Aaron's and Agnes's comments about the importance of the community, Fred scheduled speakers from the village during the entire second week. Knowing how ingrained the sexual stereotypes were in the village, Fred alternated male and female speakers, so that neither the girls nor the boys would be bored. He had anticipated some difficulty in locating some of the career role models which he thought were representative of each of the sexes, but he actually found a wealth of choice in the village. For the boys, he had asked these men to come in and talk about their jobs: Rudy Beluga, who was manager of the store; one of the young men involved with the National Guard; a pilot from one of the Salmonville air services (if he was able to); the foreman of the construction crew building a new clinic; Aaron Pete, whom the students knew since he was a teacher from the community; and two of the elders from the council. For the girls, he had asked one of the assistant cooks; the health aide from the clinic; one of the store clerks; Agnes Johnson, who taught kindergarten in Tutuluq; one of the young women in the National Guard; and two women elders.

On Thursday, Fred had asked anyone in the village whom he knew had attended at least a semester of college to come in for a group forum. Friday, as a closure of sorts, the seniors were going to write essays on "My Plans After High School."

Fred looked at the bulletin board. **"DON'T JUST DO IT FOR YOURSELF—DO IT FOR YOUR FUTURE—DO IT NOW."** He picked up the copies of his lesson plans and went in to give them to the principal and to explain what he hoped to accomplish.

"So you see," Fred concluded, not quite sure how Paul Best was taking his explanation of the project, "I'm hoping to get them involved in deciding on what it is they want to do after they graduate. I've tried using time after class, but so far I've met with limited success."

"I think it's great, Fred," Paul reassured him. "It looks to me as though you've gone to a lot of preparation for this. The only qualms I would have would be that your lesson plans might not reflect some language arts skills, and from looking at them I can see that they do. You have my full support!"

Fred breathed a little easier. "Well, I think next week a lot of Yup'ik will be spoken and only a little English."

"Again, all I ask is that your lesson plans reflect English language skills," the principal said. "For instance, I would say that there will be a lot of listening comprehension. You've set up something quite valuable for the seniors. Would you mind if I dropped in one of these days to see how it goes?"

"Of course not. Please, feel free," Fred replied.

After leaving Paul's office with his complete support, Fred wished he had told Paul earlier.

The seniors liked the bulletin board Fred had made. Most were enthusiastic about filling out the *Financial Aid Forms*, and after a few rounds of "Do what? It. You know, do IT! Yeah, let's do it right here!" they got to work.

As they filled out the FAF, step by step, Fred kept reiterating the importance of having their parents fill out their income tax forms. "Have them come talk to me or call me if they have questions with this section. But you have to get them to fill it out or you won't be able to get the money you are going to need. And remember, without the FAF, you won't be able to get the scholarship from Asiqtuq Corporation."

Half of the seniors thought that their parents had never filed taxes before. Fred told them he would be glad to help any of them with their taxes. The Asiqtuq Corporation forms were easier to understand, and the seniors could work on them independently.

On Wednesday, Thursday, and Friday the students went through the AKCIS system and used the computer disk to find out more about their career interests. By Friday, Isaac had written three letters of inquiry to aviation schools. Nathan still hedged on writing a letter, and had only filled out the FAF under duress. By the time Rudy Beluga, manager of the store, arrived Friday, neither Nathan nor Myrna had written a letter.

Fred had come to regard Rudy as a respected friend. He appreciated Rudy's sense of humor and marveled at his impeccable English. It seemed to Fred that this man was a perfect blend of modern Western culture and traditional Yup'ik culture. He had gone bird hunting with him on a couple of occasions at Rudy's invitation. Fred had spoken with Rudy about the path which seniors should follow and asked that he come speak to them and give them some advice. Rudy eagerly accepted Fred's invitation.

Rudy's speech (he agreed to speak in English) to the students focused on the uncertainty of their futures and the uncertainty of the future of Yup'ik people. He urged them to take the opportunity to pursue a course of action after high school so that they might better serve the village in the future. He also pointed out that just as in the old days, each of them had the responsibility to contribute as best they could to insure the survival of the Yup'ik people. Rudy concluded his talk with moving words, "You are wasting your precious lives if you don't take the fullest advantage of this gift of a high school in your very own village. We don't know the future. How could we? When I was your age how could I have known that this [gesturing beyond the classroom] was what it would be like? Take the skills you learn here and do something to make Tutuluq even better."

The students listened intently to Rudy. Fred felt the seniors were interested in the future of the Yup'ik people. It gave relevance and purpose to their own futures. The second week of the project with its representative Yup'ik voice, Fred felt, would be the impetus he had hoped would motivate his reluctant seniors.

The first three days of the second week went better than Fred had hoped. All the participants—except the pilot—arrived on schedule. While Fred understood very little of elders' speech, he felt certain they had made no mention of school being worth nothing. From the translations he got from Mary after the four elders left on Wednesday, it seemed that they had mostly talked about the past.

For the college forum on Thursday, Paul Best came and Aaron Pete brought his junior algebra class! Then the panelists arrived—seven women and three men. Each told about their college experience and then the students asked questions. College students still home for the Christmas break got the most questions—mostly about what college life was like and what it was like to live outside the village. The very spirited fifty minutes was not nearly enough time. Paul told him it had been "just excellent," and some of the students said, "Let's do it again tomorrow."

On Friday students moaned and groaned about having to work so hard, but each of the seniors did complete an essay on their specific plans after high school. For

Fred, the sight of his seniors working at the computers was the ultimate satisfaction.

Most of his worries about the project had been needless. All the seniors had gotten something out of it. The principal had been supportive. The role models had arrived and brought purpose and relevancy to the seniors. The elders hadn't undermined the notion of school. Fred was sorry it was over. It was up to the seniors now.

The Next Week

Fred scheduled an after-school guidance meeting for the next Tuesday. Attendance was poor. Deadlines were drawing near and the seniors knew it. Fred was puzzled and disappointed, but he was starting to accept the fact that not every senior was going to get involved. The meeting did bring one surprise though. Three young men from the community came in and asked for FAF forms and how to go about getting into the University of Alaska in Fairbanks. Fred took great delight in helping them word letters of inquiry.

In the weeks that followed, more of the villagers asked Fred for loan forms and advice. Fred called Juneau to have more FAFs and state loan applications sent. Fred was baffled. Why the sudden interest in college? Had it been there all along in a latent stage? What words had traveled through the village grapevine which brought about these sudden requests for advice? Was it a result of the project? Fred was surprised and excited.

As the semester moved on, Mary decided for certain that she wanted to get into the nursing program offered at SCC. Fred was relieved she had not chosen the military and helped her work on her entrance essay. Eva was still going to UAF. She was the first to receive a letter of acceptance. Fred could barely control his exuberance. He wished he had had a contest among the seniors to see who would get the first acceptance letter. A little competition was always beneficial to achieving results, but it didn't matter now. Adeline had finally decided that she, too, would go to UAF. Isaac was still pursuing aviation and had received replies from two flight schools in Anchorage. Nathan had changed his mind from doing nothing to getting a job in the village. Nick still had not completed all his paperwork. Myrna hadn't made any decisions. Emil had fallen so behind in his attendance that Fred and the rest of the staff decided that another home visit was necessary. Paul Best took on the responsibility of seeing if he could impress on Emil's grandfather the importance of keeping Emil from going out hunting in lieu of attending classes.

Deadlines Approaching

With the deadline for sending in the FAF nearing, Fred continually questioned his seniors as to whether their parents had finished their income tax forms. Adeline's father arrived with his tax form and Adeline's FAF form. Fred spent the evening helping him to get the forms filled out. Another victory!

Isaac came to Fred one afternoon with his acceptance letter from UAF.

"Congratulations!" Fred said. He felt ecstatic.

Isaac wasn't smiling. "I don't think so," he said.

"What do you mean? You're going to become a world famous pilot!"

Isaac laughed. "I don't know about this form," he replied, holding out his FAF.

"Is your father having trouble filling it out?"

"He said he's not going to fill it out."

Fred read the disappointment in Isaac's eyes. "Would you like me to come and talk to him?"

"I don't know."

"When would be a good time?" Fred asked, pushing.

"I don't know."

"Maybe tomorrow after school?"

"I don't think my dad wants me to leave," Isaac said. "He wants me to be around to help out."

"What about your brother. Can't he help while you're gone?"

"He's lazy," Isaac said, shaking his head.

Fred decided he was going to speak to Isaac, Sr. whether Isaac wanted him to or not. He knew how much Isaac wanted to become a pilot. "Well, listen. I'm going to come by tomorrow and talk with your father and tell him why you need to go to college. Would that be all right with you?"

"I guess so," Isaac said.

"Will you translate or would you like me to bring someone else?"

"I think maybe someone else. I'm not too good at that."

"Hey, Isaac," Fred said as Isaac turned to leave, "don't give up yet."

"Sure."

Isaac's father was one of the most respected elders in Tutuluq. Fred was a little nervous about going to talk to him. Fred spoke to Aaron Pete about Isaac's dilemma and asked him to come with him to translate the next afternoon. His hope was that Aaron's presence might be influential.

Isaac, Sr. was taking a nap when Fred and Aaron arrived. Isaac woke his father up and brought out some tea.

Fred thought it best to get right to the point. He looked at Isaac, Sr. and said, "Isaac wants to be a pilot."

The elder Isaac looked at Aaron as he translated Fred's words. He then replied, looking at Aaron, "I have a fine son."

"Yes," Fred replied. "You do. He's one of my best students. Next year he needs to go away to school so that he can become a pilot. Do you understand what this is for?" Fred pulled out the FAF form and laid it on the table.

Cross-Cultural Counseling • 43

Isaac, Sr. looked at the form and then to Aaron. "You are doing a very good job at the high school. The students learn good things there. There are things to learn from the tundra too. I know this paper. There seem to be many things to learn for the young people of today. The students need to learn about living on the tundra, not just the new education. So much is important."

Fred looked at Aaron as he translated, then said, "This is true, there are many important things, especially today. To me it is important that Isaac use the opportunity he has earned to go to college. If he waits too long, he may lose the opportunity."

"My son will go away one day." Isaac, Sr. picked up the FAF. "I need some time to think about the things you have said. They are good things and they need some consideration."

Fred left feeling very confused. He could understand Isaac, Sr.'s point of view. Or he thought he could. But at the same time his disappointment for Isaac wasn't something he would be able to shake off easily. Fred made a point to speak to Rudy Beluga to see if he could influence Isaac's father.

A flurry of activity occurred in the final days before the postmark deadline for the *Financial Aid Forms* arrived. Fred spent the afternoons helping out villagers who had last minute questions. When the dealine arrived, only Mary, Eva, and Adeline had completed and mailed their forms.

Graduation arrived, and Fred watched as the seniors walked up to receive their diplomas. Emil had dropped out of school completely. Jerry, after squeaking by the fall semester in all of his classes, had dropped out also. Mary, in her valedictorian speech, thanked Fred for helping her get into college.

Before school closed, Fred brought the AKCIS system into his junior English class. He spent four days familiarizing them with the cross-referencing and introducing the computer program. With next year's seniors, he vowed, he would start earlier, and he would do better.

Epilogue: The Graduating Seniors

Mary, the valedictorian, attended Salmonville Community College. She is still enrolled and doing well.

Adeline and Eva went to the University of Alaska Fairbanks. Eva has begun her sophomore year. Adeline completed the first semester and then decided to take some time off and live at home.

Myrna stayed in Tutuluq and lives there with her family.

Isaac lives in Tutuluq and take correspondence courses in aviation. He is currently the main provider for his parents. Like his father, he takes an active role in community affairs.

Nick had planned to attend a technical school. However, he found employment in Salmonville during the summer following graduation and moved there.

Nathan got a job with the city in Tutuluq. He is currently working in a maintenance position and is an active hunter.

Fred Young left Tutuluq after the next school year and moved outside Alaska. He is planning to return.

Discussion Questions

1. Fred Young, as site counselor at Tutuluq, has set for himself a clear goal: "motivating his seniors to do something the year following their graduation: attend a trade school, go to college, or even join the military."

A year later, two of his nine seniors, both young men, had dropped out of school entirely. Of the other three young men, one is taking correspondence courses at home, one is working in a nearby community, and one has employment at home. Of his four senior women, three have gone on to college, and one is living at home.

How would you evaluate Fred Young's success? How does Fred Young himself feel about it? Are you troubled by the goal Fred Young set for himself? What troubles you about it?

2. This case raises difficult issues of professional judgment and where to "draw the line." Do you see Fred Young as a teacher who is admirably assuming his responsibilities (rather than blaming poor outcomes on the students and community) or as a teacher who is overly ego involved in what he wants to accomplish? Fred himself worries about this problem: "was the real purpose of the project just to gratify his own ego?" How would you answer Fred's question?

Does Fred handle well the dilemma of "encouraging" versus "pressuring" Yup'ik students? Fred discusses this problem with the other guidance counselors, Barbara and Bertha. "You have to push them just enough," Barbara concludes. "If you push kids too much into something they find out they don't want to be into, they'll be bitter and blame you. If you don't push kids enough and they don't get their financial forms and admissions papers in on time, they and their parents will also blame you."

Do you think that Fred Young draws the line in the right place with his nine seniors? Is he appropriately encouraging and motivating them or is he pressuring them and trying to impose his values on their lives? Read over his specific conversations with a) Jerry, when he came back to school after not completing any of his courses when he transferred to the school in another village, b) Charlene, when he found out she was baby-sitting her sister's children rather than going to college, c) Isaac, Sr., when he found out that Isaac, Sr. would not permit his son to leave the village for college. Which of these meetings do you think Fred Young handled well? What would you have said in these situations or would you have said anything at all?

In Yup'ik communities, delicate matters are traditionally handled by indirection, rather than direct confrontation. Communicating indirectly about conflicts and problems promotes group harmony and solidarity. One traditional method of indirect communication is the use of intermediaries who convey messages. Another method is the subtle and careful way Isaac, Sr. handled the conversation with Fred Young. Do you think Fred Young would have been well advised to use a more culturally congruent style of communication in his discussions with Jerry, Charlene, or Isaac, Sr.? Or would his attempt to match Yup'ik communication styles be out of character and make him seem false and unauthentic?

3. Why is the guidance counselor role so difficult in Yup'ik communities?

Consider the adult roles that Tutuluq students want and see open to them. Does college attendance and high school success help them achieve what they want as adults? The transition to adulthood is a difficult period for many rural students (see note 1). What is causing the difficulties?

Consider the messages Tutuluq students receive about desirable futures and essential values from different socializing agents: elders in the community, the younger generation of managers and leaders like Rudy Beluga, and teachers like Fred Young. Do these messages harmonize or conflict? In what position does this leave students like the Tutuluq seniors?
College attendance rates for Alaska Native students are low, especially for young men. Native men tend to be more interested in village lifestyles than Native women are (see notes 2 and 3). In Tutuluq, three of the four young women but none of the young men to go on to college. Why are young women in communities like Tutuluq choosing different futures from young men and what are the implications for the vitality of Yup'ik communities? Does this difference affect the way guidance counselors should look at their roles?

Do you see the role of guidance counselor as different in a village like Tutuluq from what it would be in an urban area like Anchorage? If you believe the guidance role should be different in Tutuluq, how should it be different and why?

4. Fred Young tried two major approaches as guidance counselor in Tutuluq. In the fall, he encouraged students to refer to the catalogs and other print material in the counseling center, and he held after-school guidance counseling sessions. In January, he developed a special project during school hours where community people and college students came to talk to the seniors.

The second approach worked much better. Students were excited, and the principal was impressed. Community people sought Fred Young out, asking for admissions forms and advice. Exactly what was it about the second approach that made such a difference? What have you learned from Fred's experience that might affect the way you planned a guidance program for next year? Did Fred seem to learn from his experience?

Fred Young left Tutuluq after one more school year. If you replaced him as teacher and site guidance counselor, what goals would you set? What type of guidance counseling program would you develop?

In considering your own approach, think not only about Fred's failures and successes but also about other approaches used in Alaska's small rural high schools to offer guidance counseling, broaden students' experience, and increase their interest in and attachment to college (see notes 1, 4, 5, and 6).

5. Fred presents a list of questions to the school staff at the end of a meeting after a long and tiring day:
    a. What are we preparing our students for upon completion of high school?
    b. Should we encourage our graduates to remain in the village or to pursue choices outside the village?
    c. How can we best encourage the seniors to involve themselves in their futures?
    d. What is the best way to keep Yup'ik traditions alive in our students?

Are these the right questions for school faculty to be raising in Tutuluq or are these questions (or some of them) more properly the province of individual parents or the community? Try to put yourself in the place of a parent in Tutuluq. How would you react if you knew that the school faculty were discussing these questions in a staff meeting?

Fred Young is going it alone in Tutuluq. Do you see any way for Fred Young and the school to create a partnership with the parents of his seniors and the community of Tutuluq in addressing such issues? Could the community, together with the school, develop an approach to guidance? What process would you suggest that might help this happen? What risks does your approach entail?

Supplementary Materials

Note 1.
Rural Students and the Transition to Adulthood

Source: Kleinfeld, Judith, McDiarmid, G. Williamson, & Hagstrom, David. (1985). *Alaska's small rural high schools: Are they working?* (pp. 139–144). Anchorage: University of Alaska, Institute of Social & Economic Research and Center for Cross-Cultural Studies.)

The Issue

The village high schools create an exceptionally safe and nurturing environment for rural young people. Is this environment too safe and too nurturing to prepare students for making their own way as adults?

Many Students Hang Around Home After High School

After listening to rural Native high school students talk about their school experience at a statewide conference, one experienced rural educator expressed a common view:

> They are not being challenged enough. They are not being pressed hard enough, not by their teachers and not by their parents.
>
> The generation is floating. Students in these high schools don't have any clear idea of how they are going to make a living. They have no vision of the future. They didn't need one a generation ago, but now people in their twenties and thirties are just sitting at home, bored to tears. They don't like themselves.

A Native teacher, doing a case study of what happened to the graduates of small high schools in her community, reached a similar conclusion. She pointed out that the situation was worse for the young men than for the young women.

> Since the high school program began, there have been forty-nine graduates. Of these, fourteen have gone on to college and two to a seminary. All have returned home after a year or less except for one seminary student. They have returned for various reasons: homesickness, lack of preparation, and no money are the three main ones.
>
> Of the forty-nine graduates, thirty-two are males. All the young men are single and staying at home. Many of them complain about nothing to do in the village but do nothing to change their situation.
>
> Of the seventeen females, twenty-three percent are married and twenty-three percent are single with a child. The young women do not talk about being bored as much as the young men and are not as involved with drugs and alcohol.

Other statistics on high school graduates point to the same problems. One rural school district, for example, did a careful follow-up study of the 1980 to 1982 graduates of its small high schools. It found:

> Only twenty-nine percent of the responding graduates indicated that they were presently employed. In some villages, employment is zero percent. Even for the graduates that are employed, forty percent stated that they were working less than one-half the time.[22]

Small high schools have not caused the difficulties which rural students experience in making a transition to adulthood. The same difficulties occurred during the boarding school era.

Indeed, in the boarding school era, many people blamed the boarding schools for the problem: the reason young adults just hung around home after high school, the argument went, was that the boarding schools had taken them out of the village during the crucial adolescent years. Students acquired tastes for modern conveniences at boarding school, but they did not acquire the skills and dispositions necessary to satisfy these tastes. Because they were away from the village during adolescence, the students had not learned subsistence skills. Many were caught between two cultures—but were comfortable or competent in neither.

The high school—whether it is a village school or a boarding school—is not the main cause of the difficulties some rural students have in finding a satisfying adult role. The situation has many causes: the shortage of wage work in rural Alaska; dislocating cultural change; the discrimination and victimization that young people encounter in the city; pressures from parents and peers to remain in the village; and the difficulty young Native people have in identifying desirable role models (Exhibit U).

The small high schools have not caused the problem, but they are not helping to solve it either. If we take a broad view of the socialization system our society has organized for rural young people, we see a high school period characterized by intense nurturing and support, followed by an abrupt withdrawal of support at graduation. During high school, students learn in a small, personalized setting with a helpful teacher close by. After high school, students are thrown on their own.

---

[22] Carlson, Richard E. (1989, May 24). *Report on the district-wide graduate follow-up study of the classes of 1980, 1981, and 1982.* Unalakleet, AK: Bering Strait School District.

For urban as well as rural young people, the early adult years are a difficult stage of life. As Levinson shows in his study of adult development, it is a myth that urban young people settle down in their early twenties.[23] Most of them explore, experiment, and flounder around until they are close to thirty years of age.

Many village young people lack the support that their urban counterparts can count on during this difficult early adult period. Village young people are much less likely to have an uncle who can call in a favor and get them a job. They are much less likely to have a father whose business they can always fall back on. They are much less likely to have parents who know the system; who have thought seriously about their child's particular constellation of talents and limitations; and who can give guidance, emotional, and financial help during the young adult years.

Exhibit U

An Interview with the Mother of a Rural High School Graduate

Jimmy's mother cleared away a place at the kitchen table so I could interview her for the Small High School Project. Jimmy was sprawled in a recliner in the living room, watching an afternoon soap opera on television.

Jimmy is twenty years old, a graduate of a small high school. He spent his freshman through junior years at an Anchorage high school, however, before the family moved back to the community.

I started to ask his mother about the advantages and disadvantages of small high schools. Jimmy got up, flipped off the television set, and walked out.

Jimmy's mother used the interview to vent her frustration, not about the small high schools (which she thought well of), but about Jimmy's situation. He didn't want to live at home, his mother explained, but he didn't want to leave home either. His entire family lived nearby. She pointed down the street toward the homes of each of her sisters and brothers and all of Jimmy's cousins.

That summer, Jimmy had worked for a month repairing the village water system. When that job ended, he went to Anchorage and worked for four months at an auto parts store. He got laid off. When his money ran out, he came home.

"The kids come back home, and they've lost all their confidence," his mother said. "They get seventy dollars in their pocket, drive to Anchorage, party, watch TV in a motel room, and come back home. What's the sense of that?"

"He tried to get into electrician's school," she continued, "but the test required math. Now he wants to go to heavy equipment operator school, but that's real expensive."

"Our biggest problem," she said, "is the young adults. The high school kids look at the young adults and wonder if they themselves have any future."

---

[23] Levinson, Dan. (1978). *The seasons of a man's life.* New York: Alfred A. Knopf.

A Promising Strategy for Helping Rural Students Make the Transition to Adulthood: The Postsecondary Counselor in the School District Office

Rural schools have developed few strategies for helping rural young people make the transition to adulthood. This is understandable. The immediate problems of constructing high school buildings, developing a districtwide curriculum, and establishing sound programs in unconventional circumstances have absorbed the attention of rural districts. In addition, the high school as an institution does not traditionally take responsibility for students after graduation.

We did find, however, an exceptionally promising approach in one district—a postsecondary counseling program. The postsecondary counselor, located in the district office, opens a file on students when they are about to graduate from high school. The counselor shows students how to fill out the maze of college admission forms and financial aid applications. (He also keeps copies for himself in case the students lose them.)

The counselor accompanies students to interviews for apprenticeship programs. He talks to them about the impression they are making if, for example, they come to an interview with liquor on their breath. He visits students on campus and interprets students' reactions to people who do not know them. ("This psychologist thought the kid was nuts because he looked at an ink blot and said he saw someone skinning an animal. I had to tell the psychologist that, in the Bush, it's normal to skin animals.")

Students at college who need advice telephone the counselor during a crisis, sometimes during the middle of the night. College staff call him to get background information on students having problems. The postsecondary counselor also routinely visits the students away at school, as well as their relatives in the villages, reassuring everyone that everything is all right.

We came to call this postsecondary counselor program the "Freelance Father" program because the counselor resembled a cautious father—eager to help but anxious not to interfere, alternately bolstering students and bawling them out.

The program's initial success was impressive. Of the 154 district graduates who enrolled in postsecondary institutions during the two years of the program, only fifteen percent dropped out.

In this district, the postsecondary counselor works primarily with students going on to higher education. The approach could also be used, however, to help rural students find employment and help them through the rough spots on a job.

Postsecondary counseling adds one more burden to an already overburdened school system. Rural school districts, however, do occupy a strategic position to provide this type of assistance. Experienced school staff typically know the students well—their abilities, personalities, and family situations. School staff also know how the postsecondary system works and how to locate jobs. Few other rural institutions enjoy the stability, the financial resources, the expertise, and the legitimacy of the schools.

Note 2.
College Entrance Rates in Alaska by Ethnicity and Gender

Source: Kleinfeld, Judith, Gorsuch, Lee, & Kerr, Jim. (1988). *Minorities in higher education: The changing north. Alaska* [a report prepared by the Institute of Social and Economic Research in cooperation with the Western Regional Office of the College Board]. New York: College Entrance Examination Board.

- Alaska Natives are substantially underrepresented in enrollment in both two-year and four-year institutions. While Alaska Natives in 1980 comprised sixteen percent of the population, they accounted for less than six percent of enrollment at two-year institutions and less than eight percent of enrollment at four-year institutions.

- Whites are represented in enrollments in both two-year and four-year institutions in proportions greater than their proportions in the population. Every other Alaska ethnic and racial group—Blacks, Asians, and Hispanics—are enrolled in proportions less than their proportions in the population.

- Among Alaska Natives, females are enrolled in both two-year and four-year institutions in much greater proportions than males. Among Alaska Native females in 1980, 1,700 were enrolled in four-year programs compared to 1,036 Native males. In two-year programs, 1,756 Native females were enrolled compared to 882 males.

- The disparity in higher education enrollments between Native males and females increased in 1982 and increased again in 1984 (data not shown). In 1984, 2,756 Native females were enrolled in four-year programs compared to 1,408 Native males, and 2,059 Native females were enrolled in two-year programs compared to 1,021 Native males. In short, about double the numbers of Native females were enrolled in both two-year and four-year programs.

Note 3.
Participation of Inupiat Men and Women in the Wage Economy

Source: Kleinfeld, Judith, Kruse, Jack, & Travis, Robert. (1983). Inupiat participation in the wage economy: Effects of culturally adapted jobs. *Arctic Anthropology, 20*(1), 1–21.

Introduction

This study examines the response of North Slope Inupiat to large numbers of high paying local job opportunities partially adapted to Inupiat cultural patterns. These jobs were created by a local Inupiat government, the North Slope Borough, using tax revenues from Prudhoe Bay oil properties on Alaska's North Slope.

North Slope Inupiat Labor Force Patterns Compared to National Norms

Compared to national patterns, substantial differences occurred in Inupiat male and female responses to North Slope job opportunities. Surprisingly, Inupiat women participated in the labor force almost as much as women nationally. In 1977, Inupiat women had an annual labor force participation rate of 52% compared to a national female labor force participation rate of 61%. In the regional center, where job opportunities were more abundant, the Inupiat female labor force participation rate reached 62%. Those Inupiat women who did not choose to work in the wage economy tended to be a group of older women from the smaller villages who did not speak English during the interview. However, village women who spoke English during the interview were in the labor force an average of 6.7 months, about as much as women from the regional center, who averaged 7.3 months of labor force participation.

Only about 26% of Inupiat women did not work for wages in 1977. As with women nationally, the major reason (84%) Inupiat women gave for not working outside the home was family pressure and responsibility. As one explained, "My husband doesn't want me to work—just take care of the kids. I've been wanting to go to work but he won't let me."

In contrast to Inupiat women, the labor force participation of Inupiat men in the prime working ages differed substantially from national patterns. While an annual average of 91% of U.S. men aged 18–54 are in the labor force, the annual average labor force participation of North Slope Inupiat men in this age group was 58%, less than two-thirds the national average. Inupiat men in the regional center participated in the labor force only somewhat more (62%) than men living in the villages (53%).

This pattern did not occur because large numbers of Inupiat men chose not to work at all in the wage economy. Very few Inupiat men (10%) were nonwage earners. The largest proportion (41%) of these stated that health problems prevented them from working, while another 34% reported that they were laid off or could not find work. Rather, the major reasons for the comparatively low rate of Inupiat male labor force participation was that about half of Inupiat men in 1977 participated in the cash economy intermittently. During 1977, on the average, somewhat less than a third of the Inupiat male workers were temporarily withdrawn from the labor force (Table 1).

	Males (%)	Females (%)
In Labor Force		
Employed	46	44
Unemployed, wanted work	12	8
Total	58	52
Not in Labor Force		
Intermittent workers	32	22
Nonwage earners	10	26
Total	42	48
Number of Respondents	(129)	(109)

TABLE 1.
Annual Average Labor Force Participation of North Slope Inupiat Males and Female 18–54, in 1977. SOURCE: ISER North Slope Survey, 1977.

Basis of North Slope Inupiat Male Pattern of Labor Force Participation

There are two reasons for the comparatively low rate of Inupiat male labor force participation in the wage economy. The most important is economic. Despite the North Slope Borough's efforts to provide "full" employment, there was a lack of job opportunities during certain seasons and in certain villages. The second is the personal preference of about half the Inupiat male population for an intermittent work cycle. The effects of both these factors were evident in 1977, when a summer job boom followed a winter of poor job opportunities.

Due to temporary financing difficulties in the winter of 1976–1977, the Borough cut back its construction program. Intensive construction work resumed in the summer of 1977. This increase in job opportunities between the winter and summer resulted in a large increase in Inupiat male labor force participation. While only 47% of Inupiat men participated in the labor force in November 1976, 74% of Inupiat men were in the labor force in September 1977.

However, even during the summer months of abundant, high paying jobs, Inupiat male labor force participation still remained well below national norms. In the regional center during the intense 1977 summer construction season for example, labor force participation peaked at 76% of 18–54 year old Inupiat men.

When asked about their work schedule preferences, slightly over half of Inupiat men said that they preferred to work in the wage economy only part of the year (Table 2). The high paying blue-collar construction work available on the North Slope provided men with this job flexibility. Interestingly, about the same proportion of Inupiat women also preferred part-year work. However, Inupiat women primarily held white-collar jobs requiring conventional work schedules. While 60% of Inupiat female workers were employed on a year-around basis, only 39% of Inupiat male workers were employed year-around.

The preference of many Inupiat men for part-year work does not appear to be changing in the younger generation (Table 2). In a survey of North Slope high school students, more than half of the males also preferred part-year work schedules (Kleinfeld & Kruse, 1977). In contrast, Inupiat female high-school students, especially in the villages, were significantly more likely than male students to want to work year-around.

The dominant explanation in the research literature for the intermittent participation of northern men in the wage economy is desire to participate in subsistence activities. The time requirement for wage work is thought to conflict with the time required for hunting. Our analyses of the way North Slope Inupiat men allocated their time in the subsistence and wage economy suggest that this explanation requires modification. Time conflicts between hunting and wage work may indeed explain withdrawal from wage work in some situations, for example, when the work is located outside the region or when employers do not give subsistence leave. As one young Inupiat man described why he had quit his pipeline job, "I worked until April '76. It was whaling time and I came home. I told them they didn't have enough dollars to keep me working." The North Slope Borough economy, however, provided local jobs and major employers granted subsistence leave. When asked why they had left their jobs, only 4% of Inupiat men said they quit work to hunt, and they were all 18–24 year olds. Moreover, we found no relationships in our survey analyses between withdrawing from wage work and subsequently higher participation in subsistence activities.

Carrying out a high level of subsistence activities does not necessarily require long periods away from wage work. Modern hunting technology—snowmachines, rifles, outboard motors, and CB radios—has greatly reduced the time requirements. No longer must large amounts of time be spent traveling to good hunting areas or in the painstaking construction and repair of equipment. Subsistence activities can be actively pursued on weekends, after work, and on vacations and leave time. Indeed, half or more of the North Slope Inupiat adults surveyed participated in central subsistence activities on this part-time basis.

North Slope Inupiat men who work in the wage economy nonetheless maintain high levels of subsistence activity. Indeed, Inupiat men who worked in the wage economy most of the year and those who worked shorter time periods differed very little in their level of subsistence activities, and none of these differences reached statistical significance (Table 3). Among Inupiat men who worked 9–12 months per year in the wage economy, 52% maintained medium to high levels of subsistence effort. Among men who worked only 1–4 months, 45% maintained similarly high levels of subsistence activities.

In interpreting these patterns, it is important to keep in mind that the measure of subsistence activity used in the survey was crude. The interview asked if the person participated in each subsistence activity and whether or not that participation was "most of the time." The interview did not ask, for example, how many days or hours the person spent in the activity. Nonetheless, these results raise questions about the common assumption that a time conflict between wage work and subsistence is the central explanation for intermittent wage work patterns.

	Residence (%)					
	Barrow		Villages		Total	
Preferences	Males	Females	Males	Females	Males	Females
North Slope Adults						
Year-round Job	28	44	48	45	42	45
Part of Year Job	72	56	48	49	56	52
No Job	—	—	4	6	2	3
Respondents	(36)	(34)	(77)	(49)	(113)	(83)
North Slope High School Students						
Year-round Job	46	67	18	50	31	59
Part of Year Job	54	33	82	50	69	41
No Job	—	—	—	—	—	—
Respondents	(35)	(51)	(40)	(48)	(75)	(99)

TABLE 2.
Wage Work Preferences of North Slope Inupiat Adults, 18–54, and North Slope Inupiat High School Students, by Residence and Sex: 1977.

*Significant male and female differences at the $p < 0.01$ level.
Sources: ISER North Slope High School Survey, 1977; ISER North Slope Survey, 1977.

If time conflicts between wage work and subsistence are not the central explanation, what else might be important? One possibility is the historical experience of Inupiat men in the wage economy, the wage work patterns that have become customary on the North Slope. Wage work patterns of North Slope Inupiat men from the turn of the century onward reinforced the intermittent work rhythms of the traditional hunting economy. During the commercial whaling economy (c. 1854–1906), whalers competed strenuously for the labor of Inupiat crew members, particularly skilled harpooners (Sonnenfeld, 1957). For a six week's whaling season, the Inupiat crew and their families were supported through the remainder of the year by provisions of food, clothing, and housing.

Inupiat men's first widespread experience with wage work unrelated to hunting and trapping occurred through the Department of the Navy's oil exploration program in Naval (National) Petroleum Reserve #4 between 1946 and 1953 (Sonnenfeld, 1957). Barrow Inupiat petitioned for construction employment, and the Navy agreed that its civilian contractor, Arctic Construction (ARCON), would employ local labor. Inupiat men received union wages with time and a half for overtime. The work required a seven-day, nine-hour time schedule, and layoffs occurred frequently. The majority of Inupiat men worked twenty-five months out of the possible eighty-seven-month work period (Sonnenfeld, 1957).

The end of ARCON brought a period of severe unemployment, but Defense and Early Warning (DEW) Line construction began within a year. In his study of DEW-Line employment at Kaktovik, Chance (1966) found a pattern similar to ARCON employment—high demand for Inupiat labor, high wages, desire on the part of the Inupiat to participate in wage work, and a successful work adaptation combined with some intermittent work patterns. In the late 1960s, a series of uncoordinated government construction projects (schools, water supply improvements, electrical power and airport improvements, a gas distribution system, etc.) continued the boom and bust cycle (Rice & Saroff, 1964). Given these historical patterns, intermittent work at high paying jobs may have become a central adaptation of many Inupiat men to the wage economy. The current North Slope economy with its high paying, intermittent construction work is continuing this socialization experience.

Perhaps the better question is not "why do many Inupiat men prefer part-year work?" but "why would many Inupiat men want to work year-around?" Unless men are married and supporting a family (an important factor discussed later), economic pressures to work year-around are not necessarily strong. A teacher described the situation in one large North Slope village:

> I've had 23 students graduate over the last three years. Except for two working temporary construction, the others are hanging out. Last year I placed five graduates in good jobs. They drifted out over the summer. What's the incentive to work? The kids live with their parents. They get food, clothes, some spending money.

It is not clear that social prestige or sense of identity among North Slope Inupiat has much to do with one's occupational niche, as it does among middle-class whites. Our initial exploratory interviews suggest that hunting remains psychologically more important. Young men who choose intermittent work patterns discussed their wage jobs in superficial generalities but described their hunting activities in intense detail. Despite the shift from subsistence to cash as the economic foundation of contemporary life on the North Slope, the "professional" hunter, competent to survive in the Arctic, remains a central male character ideal. As one young man said of his brother:

> He's a hunter. He's always hunting. He'd be there surviving. That guy can live on anything. He's all right. He got a fox by running after it. He only works part time when he wants to make money. He's a wise man, smart.

Two characteristics distinguished those Inupiat men who chose to spend greater amounts of time in the wage economy (Table 4). The most important was being head of a family. Preservice vocational educational also made a difference but only for men who were heads of families. A North Slope Inupiat male who was not a family head and had not received vocational education was in the labor force less than half a year, an average of 5.1 months. A North Slope Inupiat male who was a family head and had vocational training was in the labor force almost twice as much, an average of 9.4 months.

Our exploratory interviews suggest that family responsibilities may increase interest in obtaining wage work. One young man said:

> Before I started this job, I decided to keep it as long as I can—then I'll be doing my hunting every chance I get. One of the reasons was I got married...

In examining the work adaptations of urban Native men, Jones (1976) similarly found that marriage was related to more stable work histories. She suggested that marriage is important not only because it brings financial responsibilities but also because it provides an important source of emotional support to men in dealing with job stress. Inupiat male labor force participation has probably not risen much, if at all, between 1960 and 1977. Inupiat female labor force participation, in contrast, has dramatically increased.

Why Inupiat Women Have Surged into the Work Force

Economic development does not necessarily increase the labor force participation of women. Quite the contrary, in many countries, the transition from a traditional to a modern economy has reduced activity of women in paid work (Durand, 1975). In some developing African nations, for example, men typically seek wage employment in mines and factories, leaving women in rural areas to tend children and work on small subsistence farms. In addition, growth of a modern commercial sector tends to hurt informal trade, a traditional sphere of African female economic activity. Colonial education systems also shut women out of the modern economic sector by neglecting the education of women in favor of preparing a small group of men for government jobs (Standing, 1976). A central theme in the research literature is the deterioration which economic development frequently brings to the economic position, status, and prestige of women (Boserup, 1970; Tinker et al., 1976). The effect of economic development on female labor force participation depends on a number of factors: the particular types of labor that are in demand, the educational levels of women, and cultural norms defining women's roles. Examining changes in female labor force participation over time in more than 100 countries, Durand (1975:120, 150) concludes:

> As economic development progresses, the overall level of participation by females in the labor force rises in some countries, falls in others, and oscillates in still others...
>
> Whether economic development brings an increase or a decrease of opportunities for women to be employed depends to a great extent on the relative proportions of female workers employed in the fields that expand and those that contract in the process of development.

The high rate of participation of Inupiat women in the wage economy results from a number of conditions. On the labor demand side, the specific type of development that has occurred on the North Slope has brought large numbers of jobs which the majority culture has conventionally defined as women's work. Since the 1960s, government has been a steadily expanding industry, and government employs large numbers of clerical, education, health, and social service workers.

On the supply side, Inupiat women have received both the general education and vocational training that qualifies them for wage work. In the younger generation, Inupiat women's level of educational attainment parallels that of men (Kruse, 1981). About a third of Inupiat women have received vocational training in paraprofessional programs and another 20% in clerical fields. Nor do Inupiat cultural attitudes toward women's roles seriously restrain female labor force participation as they do, for example, in Moslem countries with a tradition of female seclusion. The difficulties of women's role in the former subsistence economy may also have intensified Inupiat women's desires to move into the modern sector. Brower (1942:106) describes the allocation of work at the turn of the century:

> The old man hung all his whalebone on his wife's back, first lashing the butts so that the tips of the bone stuck out six feet on either side. Although the woman took it as a matter of course, it made me groan just to see her straining under the load. Not so their two full-grown sons. Hardly had they started when the boys hung their bone on her back as well. This left them with only their rifles to carry. Soon even these were a burden, so they piled them on their mother, too. It was a sight to remember—that loaded down woman followed by three husky men sauntering along with their hands behind them, at peace with the universe.

In examining the response of men and women to culture change among the Blood, Cree, and rural Germans, Spindler and Spindler (1975) point out that women tend to be less conservative than men and more interested in instrumental adaptations outside the traditional system. Economic changes on the North Slope provided Inupiat women with nontraditional opportunities. However, while Inupiat women focus a large part of their economic efforts in the wage economy, their earnings help the household maintain effort and prestige in the subsistence economy. In households where Inupiat women worked more at wage jobs, other family members spent more time in subsistence and the household shared more subsistence foods with other households (Kleinfeld et al., 1981).

Note 4.
Counseling Programs in Small Rural High Schools

Source: Kleinfeld, Judith, McDiarmid, G. Williamson, & Parrett, William. (1986). *The teacher as inventor: Making small high schools work.* Fairbanks: University of Alaska, College of Human and Rural Development.

Description

When Dorian Ross became principal of the Togiak School, he brought with him the experience of starting counseling programs in Iran and in Craig. In this program, individual teachers serve as mentors for small groups of students.

Here's how Dr. Ross' counseling period works:

Monday	carries out the theme for the month. At the beginning of the year, the theme is orientation to the junior high, the high school, or the new term. Later in the year, counselor and students focus on test-taking skills in preparation for the annual California Achievement Tests.
Tuesday	is used to develop problem-solving and decision-making skills.
Wednesday	is reserved for academic and personal guidance. The teacher-counselor checks on individual academic progress or works with students on social skills and self-image.
Thursday	is left up to the students. Some use the time for special meetings—such as the DECA club or student council. Others use it as a study hall or as an opportunity to get tutorial help from the teacher-counselor. Students may even choose to use the time for social events such as birthday parties.
Friday	is reserved for schoolwide assemblies. These could be pep rallies, talent shows, guest speakers, or special student presentations.

Dr. Ross explains that the program serves two primary purposes. Because full-time counselors are an almost unheard of luxury in small schools, teacher-counselors provide career and educational guidance and social and emotional support. Secondly, the program strengthens relationships between the student and teacher. The teacher-counselors act as "scholastic leader, trusted friend, parental stand-in, and adult model." The warmth of the relationships created through the program radiates throughout the school.

How To

1. *"Don't set rules and then expect the students to buy into them,"* advises Dr. Ross. Consult with teachers, students, and their parents.

2. *Creating counseling groups.* At least two approaches may be used in forming groups. First, students may be grouped by grade level. This approach has the advantage of familiarity; students know the others in their grade. Second, students can choose their advisor; students name their first two or three choices and the principal apportions students accordingly. This method allows cross-age relationships to develop among the students and is more like the family structure in the community. If you choose the family grouping method, Dr. Ross suggests that students be limited to two or three changes of advisors during their six years in junior and senior high school.

3. *Be flexible.* Be prepared to alter the daily schedule to take advantage of unexpected visiting talent such as an archaeologist or UAF's TUMA Theater.

4. Follow the the morning group meetings with a "cooling out" activity. For schools using traditional fifty-minute periods, Dr. Ross suggests a twenty-minute block of silent sustained reading.

With a program structured into the regular school day, teachers have the time and opportunity, often denied by the sheer "busy-ness" of schools, to keep up with what is going on with students.

Variations

- *Site Counselors:* Bering Strait School District enlists a teacher at each school site to serve as a volunteer counselor. "The key," explains Director of Curriculum/Instruction and Counseling, Richard Carlson, "is to start slowly and provide training to the teachers." The volunteers are brought into the district office for two to three days of training each year. The district counselor keeps in touch with the teacher-counselors, sending them materials on scholarships, study skills, dealing with stress, and so on.

The final step is posting notices to let parents and students know who the on-site counselor is and what his role is.

- *Career Counseling:* The lack of rural school counselors has led some teachers to devise special courses to prepare students to enter careers or postsecondary education. Dina Thain at Klawock has done just that. In her Career Class, college-bound students hone their study skills while vocational education students practice skills such as résumé writing. Dina says that, since the class began in 1982, "about sixty to seventy percent of the students are in productive fields, doing something for themselves."

Dina has her students establish goals for themselves at the beginning of the year. She shows film strips or holds audio conferences with people in various fields to inform students of the realities of different professions or trades.

Students focus their career interests through "self-esteem projects" that help them clarify their priorities and identify their strengths and weaknesses. Students also keep journals in which they record their dreams, aspirations, and autobiographical information. Finally, they keep "career notebooks" in which they record goals and values, job descriptions, their résumé, college descriptions, application forms, and other practical information.

Note 5.
Broaden Students' Experience with Travel Programs

Source: Kleinfeld, Judith, McDiarmid, G. Williamson, & Parrett, William. (1986). *The teacher as inventor: Making small high schools work.* Fairbanks: University of Alaska, College of Human and Rural Development.

In this chapter, we explore how rural teachers use the opportunity to travel with their students to:

- Broaden the students' experience of the world

- Teach the students unfamiliar concepts

- Help the students acquire a more realistic picture of contemporary American life

- Give the students an opportunity to make better judgments on what they want to do after high school

The isolation of rural villages leads small high school teachers to seek ways of broadening their students' experience of the world. Many teachers see the opportunity to travel with their students as one of the great advantages of small high schools. With 17 students, not 1,700, everything is manageable.

Some rural school districts have travel policies built around a "travel scope and sequence." Younger students go to Anchorage or Fairbanks to get firsthand experience in a city. Older students travel outside Alaska so they can better understand contemporary American life. High school seniors go on a tour of colleges and vocational schools so they can make better judgments about what to do after high school.

In other districts, teachers are on their own. Some teachers plan an entire academic year around a big study trip.

Organizing Study Trips

Ft. Yukon Students See America on a Greyhound Bus.

Description

Bill Pfisterer and Carolyn Peter, teachers at the Ft. Yukon School, met with the parents of their 36 Athabaskan students and jointly planned an across-country tour. They structured the tour around Greyhound's special 35-day Ameripass. Pfisterer, Peter, and a half-dozen parents accompanied the students. To save money, they traveled at night and slept on the bus.

They toured a furniture factory on an Indian reservation in the Southwest, saw a calf born on a Midwestern dairy farm, and didn't forget to stop at Disneyland. In Ohio, the students visited pen pals who had earlier trekked north to Alaska. They stayed in their pen pals' homes and swam in their pools.

On the East Coast, they hiked along trails in the Great Smokey Mountains and toured historical sites in Washington, D.C. When they returned to Ft. Yukon, they had more experience of the United States and its diversity than most of their counterparts in large urban schools.

The trip that Bill, Carolyn, and the Ft. Yukon parents organized illustrates the benefits of such student travel. Students experience firsthand many of the places, events, and concepts that they read about in textbooks. Such travel also helps dispel students' sense of isolation. They are able to see the similarities, as well as the differences, between their way of life and that of others. They get a much more realistic picture of the world than the one that comes across on the television screen.

Finally, travel helps students to put their own experience into perspective. They are better able to see the options and alternatives open to them. Whether they choose to stay in Ft. Yukon to fish and trap or whether they choose to leave to take a salaried job, they will have had a chance to see what is over the mountain.

How To

For the following suggestions, we are indebted to Bill Pfisterer, Glenys Bowerman, and the students of Noatak.

1. *Get ready.* At least three options are available for organizing the trip. First, you can work through a travel agent. Second, you can sign up for a prepackaged tour. Such tours are available to just about anywhere in the world. Third, you can plan the trip yourself—which is what Bill Pfisterer and Carolyn Peter did.

"Get the students involved," says Bill. Have them write to the Chambers of Commerce in the cities you are thinking of visiting. Have them contact a local high school in the city. Send the school a video of your school, the students, and the village. Have them work out a schedule, computing travel time and mileage to different cities as well as the money needed. As they are learning to arrange travel, they are also reading, writing, and calculating. Not bad for what some critics call a frill.

2. *Getting together the wherewithal.* With Indian Education and Johnson O'Malley funds, as well as oil revenues, fast drying up, self-reliance is yet another lesson students can learn from travel. Noatak students held a carnival and raised $4,000 in two nights. Nenana students have managed to raise $3,400 each during the last two years. Ft. Yukon students supplemented funds provided by the BIA to amass nearly $30,000 for their cross-country jaunt.

Here are some ideas:

Food: Yes, the ubiquitous bake-sale is tried and true—but think on a grander scale: Open a student store during recreation hours. Serve cinnamon rolls and juice in a morning "wake-up-teria." Run concessions for sporting events and cook meals for visiting teams.
Information: Put together a cookbook of local recipes and sell it. Students in Nenana collected recipes—including a sure winner, "Polar Bear Grunt Stew"—and had a local artist draw a picture for the cover. The book was printed cheaply by a printer in Tennessee.
Stage Special Events: Noatak students built booths for their Senior Carnival and ordered raffle prizes. The whole community turned out to play games, eat, and swell the travel kitty.
For more ideas, contact Glenys Bowerman at Nenana High School who has generously offered her help.

3. *Getting ready academically.* This is an opportunity for true interdisciplinary studies. In social studies, students can learn about the geography, culture, and economy of the places they are to visit. In math, they can compute expenses, mileage, and per student cost. In science, they can learn about the technology of industries and mining in the places they are to visit. In art and music, they can study regional art works, architecture, artists and composers. In English, they can write letters to inquire about the places they will visit. The possibilities are almost limitless.

4. *Setting off.* Have plenty of chaperones. Think carefully about an appropriate span of supervision. Ft. Yukon had eight adults for thirty-six students. Frank Mitchell took five adults to supervise twenty-six students from the Iditarod School District. In other words, plan for one adult for each group of five or six students.

Students should learn about how to act with strangers, how to act in public places, and how to address people in various positions. Students who are unfamiliar with traffic should learn some rules for pedestrians.

Prepare students for accidental separation. Tell them how to find the police—or in a foreign country, the American Embassy. Each student should also have an itinerary that includes the address and phone number of their lodgings for the entire trip.

(For additional information see Urban Survival Skills Programs in the last section.)

5. *During the trip.* Organize a system for accounting for students. You may want to have students wear bright sweatshirts or jackets so they can be easily spotted and can spot one another.

Before arriving at each destination, review with the students the behavior expected of them. Point out local cultural rules. Chaperones may also need this information. An outraged ranger in the Smoky Mountains apprehended a parent-chaperone who had cut down a tree to make a clothesline.

Have students take along some small, inexpensive gifts that they can give as tokens of appreciation. Nenana students ordered pins in the shape of Alaska—at a little more than a dollar each (from Stewart Photo in Anchorage). Each student had 20 pins to give away during the trip to Europe.

Students can keep journals, take photographs, and make videotapes to be shown to their community. Be sure to allot time for these activities.

6. *Follow-up.* Research demonstrates that students learn much more from out-of-school experiences if teachers create opportunities to reflect on them later in the classroom. It is the thinking about the trip that is most educational. Follow-up activities could include:

- Writing thank-you letters to people who hosted them or helped fund the trip.
- Presenting a slide show or showing videotapes for the community.
- Presenting oral reports, using visual supports such as slides or tapes, to schoolmates, teachers, parents, and the local and district school boards.

Despite the expense involved, travel is one of the most valuable educational experiences you can organize with your students. Once they and their parents get behind the idea, you are on your way.

Variations

- *A Trip to France:* In McGrath, Deane O'Dell helped organize a trip to France for all the students in the Iditarod District who were taking French in 1978. During the first three weeks of their stay, the students lived with French families and attended school. The last two weeks they toured the country—Marseille, Nice, Chamonix, Paris—relaxing on beaches, visiting fishing and mountain communities, walking through museums, and shopping.

- *A Trip to the Tribes:* In 1979, Francis Mitchell and 26 students from the Iditarod District embarked on a "Trip to the Tribes." After stopping at an Indian center in Seattle, the group rented three vans and took off for Indian territory. Traveling from reservation to reservation, the students learned about various North American Indian cultures, including the Yakima in Washington, Nez Pierce in Idaho, and the Salish, Kootenai, Blackfoot, Cheyenne, and Crow in Montana.

At the University of Montana in Missoula, students learned more about Indian history and current events from the Indian Studies Program—and got additional information from the Urban Indian Program. The grand finale was the Northwest Powwow in Tacoma.

- *A School Travel Club:* Students in Nenana worked for two years to raise the money for their month-long European tour in 1980. Thus was born the Nenana Travel Club. In addition to the first trip that included Spain, France, and England, students have raised money to tour Belgium, the Netherlands, Germany, Austria, Switzerland, Lichtenstein, Italy, Greece, and Yugoslavia. When the threat of terrorism forced them to cancel their 1986 European tour, they headed east—to Australia, New Zealand, and the Fiji Islands.

- *A Senior Tour of Colleges and Vocational Schools:* Seniors from Kwigillingok visited community colleges, vocational centers, and universities in Seward, Anchorage, Palmer, Fairbanks, and Bethel. During their one-week tour, they also visited Kenai to see the impact of oil development on that area.

Students prepared by researching the institutions they would visit, mapping their trip, and learning the jargon of colleges, stores, and restaurants. Each student also developed a list of twenty questions that they would have to ask during their tour. They also kept journals of their experiences. When they returned to Kwigillingok, they had conferences with their parents and the school counselor to discuss their career plans.

Note 6.
University Programs that Assist Rural High School Students Make the Transition to College

Source: Kleinfeld, Judith, McDiarmid, G. Williamson, & Hagstrom, David. (1985). *Alaska's small rural high schools: Are they working?* Anchorage: University of Alaska, Institute of Social & Economic Research and Center for Cross-Cultural Studies.

Several statewide programs bring rural students to a college campus during the summer both to sharpen their academic skills and to get them used to the demands of college life. These programs include (1) Upward Bound, (2) the Della Keats Health Careers Program, and (3) the Rural Alaska Honors Institute.

The Rural Alaska Honors Institute (RAHI), for example, selects academically talented juniors from rural high schools and brings them to the University of Alaska's Fairbanks campus for a six-week college experience. Students see for themselves exactly what college classes are like. They see the kinds of academic skills they will need in college at a time when they are juniors and still have another school year to prepare themselves. Students not only improve their mathematics, writing, and research skills; they also learn how to handle such demands of college as having to stand at a podium and make a formal presentation in front of an audience. Rural students also experience bouts of homesickness and loss of nerve in a short college program where the staff expects such difficulties and knows how to support students through them.

RAHI deliberately creates stressful experiences—such as a paper due the same day as a midterm exam—to simulate the pressures of college life. Students have the opportunity to learn in a protected setting exactly how they will do on an exam when they have stayed up all night to write a term paper.

Over 80 percent of the rural principals who had students in this program rated it as "very effective." Of the thirteen RAHI students who entered as freshmen at the University of Alaska, Fairbanks, campus in 1984, all thirteen completed the semester, and twelve returned for the spring semester.